SILENT WORDS:

Animals Speak from the Heart

by

Animal Communicator
CINDY WOOD
with Merry Shelburne

SILENT WORDS

ISBN number 978-0-615-28186-5

Table of Contents

Dedication

Dedicated to and in Memory of
Winston E. Woodlin
1973-1988

For letting me enter his world of silence.
For being wise enough to know I had a gift and patient enough to see
me through it.
Not only did he change my life but he also changed the lives of
many of his kind, forever.
Thank you for sharing that lifetime with me, My Little Kindred
Spirit.

When a soul from the heavens is placed back into this physical
world, it starts a ripple in life. As the ripple flows outward towards
the shoreline, it touches many lives along the way. But it is the soul
that touches so deep into our most inner self that we know we love
without question. We cannot help it. It is not a job or a chore; it is
just there.

Why is it when we see them asleep, we must kiss them awake?
Why does the human need to touch and keep that silent world
awake? What is it they have that we want? Could it be the ability to
speak from their hearts? Or is it because they are like little sponges
who take away all our anxiety and frustrations and then open their
hearts for our sadness. For when a tear falls on their fur, it never
dries. Their eyes are not blinded with love that has conditions, for
their love is the purest of all.

May the white light always be around your soul and touch the
hands that hold the animal kingdom so close to your heart.

Cindy Wood
January 2009

Foreword

A Novice's Perspective

I was sitting on the patio outside the vet's office, waiting for the acupuncturist to treat my dysplastic, eight-year-old Golden Retriever.

It was our custom to chat while Nancy worked, and I was looking forward to that day's conversation. Fuzzibear and I were there every two weeks, like clockwork.

During the previous months, Nancy had mentioned a few times that she knew an animal communicator. I like to keep an open mind, so I was always interested in what she had to say and listened carefully, trying to decide whether or not I "believed."

As I waited on the patio that day, an SUV pulled into the parking area, and a casually dressed woman with short brown hair got out of the car. She didn't have an animal with her, so I assumed she was picking up a pet.

The woman stopped to talk for a few minutes and then put her hands on either side of Fuzzibear's head and looked into his eyes.

"Yes, you have a lot of good years left in you, don't you?" she crooned to him. "Yes, you're an old soul, aren't you? Yes."

I smiled to myself, thinking she was a lovely, kind person.

And then, still looking into his eyes, she said to me, "You know, he doesn't like it when she follows him down into the yard. He likes to scout out the yard first, and then she can come down. And he'd like you to tell her that."

Without another word, the woman turned and went into the vet's office.

I sat there with my mouth open, wondering how this complete stranger knew a full flight of deck stairs led to my back yard, and how she knew I had a female dog at home.

At that moment Nancy appeared with needles in hand and settled into a chair.

I said, "Was that…?"

And she said, "Yes. That's Cindy Wood."

I told her what had transpired, but she wasn't surprised. I was still trying to understand what had happened when Cindy came back out the door and approached us.

"I have a message for you," Nancy told her. "Blacky is sleeping through the night now. As soon as they got his bed out of the draft and turned out the nightlight, he was fine."

"Great," Cindy said with a smile. She circled around behind Fuzzibear, watching Nancy work. "It really feels good when you put the needles in up here," she told Nancy, gesturing toward his upper shoulder area.

Thoughts swirled around in my head, but I was too awestruck to say anything.

They chatted about a horse who missed his "Mom," and then Cindy put her hands on Fuzzibear's rump, right above his tail.

Finally, I opened my mouth. "What is it you're feeling back there?" I asked her.

"It feels hot," Cindy said.

Nancy and I immediately pulled up his thick, curly fur. Sure enough, he was starting a hot spot.

After Cindy left, I asked Nancy about Blacky.

"He was up pacing the house all night," she said, "and it drove his 'parents' crazy. Then Cindy said he told her his doggie bed was in a draft and the light kept him awake."

I shook my head in wonder, kicking myself for not taking the opportunity to ask Cindy all kinds of questions.

When I got home I told my husband about our adventure, and he immediately began referring to Cindy as the "horse whisperer," alluding to one of our favorite Robert Redford movies.

A few months later we decided to make an appointment with Cindy. Fuzzibear was having a bad time with hot spots, and we wanted to see if we could get some insight into the cause.

I can't explain why we believed in her. I suppose it was because she was so down-to-earth and straightforward, and she had such an unpretentious way about her. She was one of those people you instantly like.

After a brief introduction, my husband took Goldie (our female Golden puppy) into the back of the house so Fuzzibear wouldn't be distracted.

Cindy told me many things on that first visit as she interpreted the pictures she was getting from our boy. He referred to my husband as "the marshmallow" and to Goldie as "the maniac." It wasn't until later that I understood how the picture trading worked and how she created words to describe the pictures. In any case, she said he was not in pain with his hips but experienced a tingling when he lay in one position for too long, and the tingling caused him to bite those spots. He also told her he hated the e-collar I was making him wear to prevent him from doing further damage to himself.

Fuzzibear wanted us to know that it hadn't been necessary to bring another dog into the house, because he had been perfectly content by himself after Woofy crossed the Rainbow Bridge the previous summer. Nevertheless, he liked Goldie and was teaching her a few jobs, like "cleaning the yard" and "putting the squirrels in the trees."

It was a memorable, eye-opening session, and one I will never forget.

During the following months, the "horse whisperer" became a member of our extended family and we introduced her to other people with dogs. Some of our friends were skeptical, but once they saw Cindy interact with their animals, all doubt was gone.

In October of 2003, Cindy asked me to collaborate on a book, because I am a writer by profession. Her reasoning was that people would treat animals with greater respect and kindness if they understood how those animals felt.

I jumped at the chance to learn more about inter-species communication and about Cindy's "gift." The information I gathered during the collaboration process helped me to be more attuned to our dogs, and I even learned how to send simple mental pictures to Fuzzibear and Goldie for the purpose of behavior modification.

Alas, try as I might, I could not receive their pictures. But we had Cindy for that.

Merry Shelburne

January 2009

Chapter 1
How It All Began

Some of my favorite childhood memories are of the concerts I gave in my mother's New Mexico sewing room. I would gather all our pets, including 14 mice, and play the violin for them. That activity was a source of comfort because it kept me "grounded" when my mind and my soul were beginning to experience little episodes of... what? I couldn't put it into words. I just *knew* things.

I was born on the Isthmus of Panama, where Dad was serving in the U.S. Army. My earliest memories are of incessant rain and lush vegetation that looked like green velvet.

When I was five, we moved to Southern California and my father went to work for U.S. Customs. What a difference in my environment! We were in suburbia: rolling hills and valleys filled with housing tracts, somewhere between the ocean and the mountains.

But the moving continued. When I was ten, we packed our bags and belongings and went to New Mexico, where Dad had a security job with Hughes. That landscape, and its bold rock formations, was vastly different from anything I had experienced before. I began to have an appreciation for the variety of scenery available on this earth, as well as the animals indigenous to those habitats.

Three years later, Hughes relocated us back to Southern California, and my father remained in the security division until he retired. I've always believed there was a reason – things I was meant to experience and animals I needed to meet – for all the moving around we did.

And there were, indeed, many animals. I was the second of five children, and our home was always filled with every kind of pet imaginable. We had dogs and cats and bunnies and turtles and more, and we loved them all.

I had a special bond with these creatures. It seemed as if I sensed what they were thinking much of the time, and I often found this troubling.

The only person who really understood my increasing concern about this issue was my paternal grandmother. She lived in New Jersey and we drove there every summer for a visit. I could hardly wait to see her, because her calming voice always comforted me as she explained how I knew certain things.

Of course she understood. She was an astrologer – a psychic to the "Stars," if you will – with a sizeable clientele from Hollywood. Many would not make a move without consulting her first. She also was involved in investigating the famous Lindberg baby kidnapping. I vividly remember her Tea Room, where her guests would gather before she "read" for them.

She was a wonderful person, and I wish I could have spent more time with her. I know she could have taught me many things and helped me through the transitions.

Dad downplayed the idea that I might have inherited his mother's gift and explained everything as "coincidences."

I believed him, with only a few reservations, until one day when I was ten.

As I sat in my fifth grade class, a sudden, severe headache overwhelmed me. The school nurse sent me home, and I was surprised to find Dad up and about. He worked the night shift at that time and normally slept during the day.

"What's wrong?" I asked.

"It's Sandy," he said.

Sandy was a blond Cocker Spaniel, and he and I were inseparable, except when I was in school. We did everything together, and nearly every day I would walk him across a nearby wash to my maternal grandparents' house.

On this particular day, Sandy had decided to visit my grandparents on his own. He was tied up in the backyard on a very long rope, and when he scampered over the wall to the wash, the rope wasn't long enough for his feet to reach the ground.

Dad explained that Sandy had accidentally hanged himself.

My headache went away instantly. And that's when I knew, in my heart of hearts, that I had inherited my grandmother's telepathic gift, albeit in a different form. She saw the future for people, while I was tuned in to the here-and-now with animals.

Dad, of course, said the headache incident was a coincidence, but I knew better. I kept that knowledge to myself. I knew instinctively that my father was trying to protect me, because sometimes working with animals can be very painful to the heart. Plus, there was a kind of stigma attached to this gift. Some people thought my grandmother was odd, and he didn't want me to suffer the same consequences.

The following year, one of our cats ran away up into the foothills. I loved Rusty dearly and was determined to recover him. It was a vast area, but somehow I knew exactly where to find my little orange ball of fur. I didn't know how I knew. I just did. And I led my brother right to him.

During the next decade there were many similar incidents, and my family acknowledged that I had inherited my grandmother's gift for non-verbal communication. My parents and siblings were supportive and nurturing and have since become my biggest fans.

But the truly life-altering event came in 1979.

My Airedale, Winston, who was only six years young, had stopped eating and drinking. The vets could find nothing wrong with him, but I was determined to get to the bottom of the problem.

Winston had jet-black ears that made him look like a giant teddy bear, and he was truly an old soul. He didn't look at you so much as he looked through you. I couldn't bear to have him put down.

So, I made an appointment with Beatrice Lydecker, a well-known animal communicator. The day before we were to see her, I was petting Winston and I got clear pictures of his jaw and a piece of wood in my mind. But there was no connection between the two pictures.

The next day, Bea asked Winston to tell her what was wrong. He showed her that he had put his paws on top of a wooden gate, had slipped, and his jaw had come down hard on the gate. She said he had a hairline fracture, a condition that did not show up on the X-rays.

Smiling to myself, I wondered if I could possibly hone my skills so that I would see the breadth of the whole picture instead of just parts of it.

I took Winston back to the vet for treatment, and we were together for nine more years.

I also signed up for a class with Bea and trained with her for three months. She taught me to step back and see the whole picture from the animal's perspective and to put what I saw into words people could comprehend.

You see, animals are constantly sending out "pictures" in their minds, trying to communicate with us, but they get no answer. They are very excited when a human can "see" their pictures and send some back, and they are more than willing to answer questions.

The biggest obstacle I had to overcome was translating the pictures sent to me by small animals. Remember how large and tall everything looked to you when you were a child? That's how little animals see things, of course, so their pictures seemed out of proportion to me and came from the wrong angle. I learned to sit on the floor with them, and that helped.

Depending on their individual personalities, some animals would come right to the point and send me a still photograph. With others, it was like watching a videotape.

I could also "feel" their emotions and sense hot and cold.

When I asked them questions, sometimes it was as if we were transported into the realm of virtual reality. For example, a Golden Retriever had been refusing the teeter-totter in her agility trials. I sent her a picture asking her to show me the apparatus, and she gave me a video – from her perspective – of traversing the teeter. I felt her hesitation due to the subtle and unintentional body language of the handler.

How do I translate the pictures into words? Here's an example:

Two poodles — a 16-years-young gray female named Pooka and a black 7-year-old male named J.J. – were sharing their lives with a widow.

J.J. showed me a "video" of moving furs. They had no heads or paws or tails, but I could tell they were squirrels. Obviously J.J. thought of them as just fur, so my translation for the squirrels was "the furs."

He wanted to put the furs away every day and didn't like them running around his yard. His Mom, however, liked to watch their antics. So, I made a compromise deal with J.J: he would leave a few in the yard each day, but he could put away (chase from the yard) the rest of them.

Meanwhile, Pooka had something to say as well. She showed me wetness all around her and I could feel her extreme comfort. I translated that to mean: "Tell my Mom that I like it when she takes me to the wets." Pooka also showed me that J.J. was not there at the groomer's shop, and she enjoyed her special time away from him.

Animals often have what we would consider odd ways of expressing themselves. But their "vision" is always pure, even if their pictures sometimes are not.

During my training period I spent many hours in vets' outer offices and in parks, in fact anywhere I thought pets might be with their human companions. I practiced and practiced, using my gift to help people understand their animals.

When I told people what their pets were feeling or thinking, some were surprised and a few were skeptical. I discovered that those who were the most affectionate and caring with their animals were the most open to the ideas I was expressing.

Frequently, I was asked questions such as "How do you know Spot sleeps in a bed by the fireplace?" or "How do you know Spot was hit by a car when he was young?" I would tell them about the mind pictures.

Sometimes, if they were really interested, I would explain to the pet owners that we were all born with the ability to communicate in this fashion. But, because language is a much more efficient way to express ourselves, we soon "lose" this skill because we don't practice it. In fact, the first humans on this earth communicated using mental pictures, long before languages were developed.

Occasionally someone would ask me how I knew that Spot was feeling happy or lonely or cold, and I would explain that I could sense the animal's emotions and physical discomforts.

This is the most painful aspect of my gift. I had to train myself not to take on the animals' feelings, for my own self-preservation. I guess I'm not as strong as animals are. Ironically, they willingly take on our emotional sadness and believe it is their purpose in life.

I also discovered that animals have senses of humor and that inter-species communication within the animal kingdom takes place on a fairly regular basis. But I'm getting ahead of myself...

After my three-month "internship" with Bea, she had to go on an extended trip to Europe; and she turned over all of her clients to me. I was at once both ecstatic and terrified. Would I be able to do the job?

I had learned that sometimes there is interference in the non-verbal animal-human communication process, just as there is in the human-human process using language. On those occasions, I had to be realistic and say, "This just isn't working today. Let me come back tomorrow." How would her clients react?

I also knew that animals never lie and I should never back away when an owner was telling me something different. What would her clients think?

As it turned out, I had no problems at all. When Bea finally returned, many of her old clients elected to stay with me. I think perhaps it was because I went to the animals' homes rather than having them come to me, because I thought they were more comfortable in their own environments. In any case, the clients' decision was a circumstance that surprised me but did not seem to surprise Bea at all.

She was my mentor, and I will be forever grateful to her.

During the next 25 years, I was employed at a regular job during the day and worked with my clients in the evenings and on weekends. In January of 2004, I became a full-time animal communicator.

One of the highlights of my part-time career was a session I had with a UCLA parapsychology class in 1981. I was invited to demonstrate my gift, and the students brought in five animals. Afterwards, Dr. Thelma Moss, the professor, wrote me a letter of commendation.

She wrote, in part:

Throughout my research in parapsychology, I have given only three letters of commendation. It is important to say this, because so many people claim to have been tested at UCLA, by me and my colleagues. Many people have been seen by us, but no one has "passed" as a psychic.

You, yourself, do not claim to have "psychic abilities." What you do profess, and what you clearly demonstrated last Wednesday, was the ability to receive accurate impressions from the five animals with whom you were presented...

The diagnosis of animals, through some kind of psi ability, has been described in the literature of parapsychology — but yours was the first example, in which I could believe...

Dr. [Jan] Berlin and I would like, with your permission, to have you as a referral source for those persons who need help with their pets...

It was wonderful to be acknowledged in that manner, but my true validation comes – every day – from the animals themselves.

In that vein, I must share one "Winston" story with you. I had covered the surfaces of his outdoor eating area with green astro-turf. He liked that. But when I had the house's interior floors covered in wall-to-wall beige carpeting, Winston went into full pout. You see, he was not consulted about the color of the carpet, and he preferred green! Once I put down some green "runners" on top of the beige, he was satisfied and returned to his normal personality. After that, I was careful to ask his opinion!

Winston was a very special little guy, but I have not been without him all this time. After he crossed to the other side, his soul reappeared a few years later in the body of an Airedale puppy named Benjamin. He showed me right away who he was and told me that he was there to support and comfort me.

Ben was a special-needs dog with many physical problems, but he helped me more than I ever helped him. He took on my emotional pain when I lost the love of my life, and Ben stayed with me until he was eight.

Winston has reappeared again, this time in the form of my current Airedale, McKenzie. We have such a long history together that we're quite comfortable with one another. Some things never change, of course. I still consult with him about colors!

Even though it's the same little soul, it's interesting to note that their personalities all have been different. For example, McKenzie has a mischievous streak that was not so apparent in the others. He's into everything. When I ask him why he has done something, invariably he answers, "Because I can!" When he was Ben, he couldn't because of his limitations.

He always seems to be buried in some shrubbery, and all I can see are his tail and hind legs as he rousts a few birds or a squirrel. One day I inquired as to why I was seeing only his backside, and he said, "Because my face is busy!"

Can there be any doubt that our animal companions provide hours of amusement as well as comfort?

For many years, my clients encouraged me to write a book that would help people truly understand their animals. I take it one step further. I've written this book to help the animals themselves, in the hope that human understanding ultimately will yield more compassionate treatment of our animal companions and their brethren in the wild.

Some of the chapters are organized by common events, such as how they feel about their food, jobs and friends. The subject of one is reincarnation, because animals sometimes tell me they have been with their owners before. Other sections are devoted to special stories that do not fit into a category.

Each tale reveals key insights into the hearts and souls who populate the animal kingdom. They often see situations so much more clearly – and purely – than we do, and we can learn a great deal from them.

It is my sincere hope that this book will bring to you both comfort and joy.

SILENT WORDS

Chapter 2
The First Puppy

About eight years after I started to communicate with animals, my beloved Winston was almost 15 years old. I knew our time together would soon be ending.

Life without a dog does not work for me. As fate would have it, the kennel where I occasionally boarded my dogs while I was traveling also bred Airedales and had four male puppies ready for new homes.

I went to visit, and it didn't take long for one of them to run over and pull a branch off a small tree. Then he ran around with it and was so proud of what he had done.

He turned to me and asked, "Is this not great?"

Well, that did it for me. He won me over. I had to wait a few more days to bring him home, and those were the longest days of my life.

So many things were running through my head. He would be the first puppy I had where we would be communicating from day one. Could we do this? How long would it take him to understand we were communicating?

Then it came to me. This was new to me, but it was the only way he knew. It would not be a problem for him.

I was so excited! As the weeks unfolded, I could see how different Maxwell was from the other puppies I'd had in the past.

We went to obedience class. After a while I stopped verbal communication and instead visualized what I needed him to do. That was great fun!

At home all I had to do was picture him in my mind and he would be right by my side. At times he would just appear, and I never heard him come into the room.

He was so into his way of communicating, and I did not realize what the consequences would be.

As he grew older, he began to exhibit signs that he did not want to be around other people unless I was with him. When I, or a close friend, would take him back to the kennel where he was born, to stay for a while and have a bath or a trim or see the vet, Maxwell would return with severely depleted enthusiasm. He didn't want to play or communicate.

One day I asked him what was wrong when he came home from the kennel.

"People don't like me," he said. "They never answer me when I ask them for something, or when I ask what they're going to do next."

It had never occurred to me that Maxwell would think all humans could communicate with animals! We had a long talk and I explained everything to him, and after that he could hardly wait to tell me what went on when we were apart.

This was such a valuable lesson for me! Ever since then, I've explained the situation to all new puppies before they even go out into the world. I tell them that most people can't communicate with them, so they can talk to me instead.

Maxwell taught me another big lesson while I was in the process of teaching one to him.

I thought he needed to know the value of sharing, so I taught him a game I called "Rope." I would hold one end of the rope and he would have the other. Sometimes I would let go, and he would happily run across the room with the rope, throw it up in the air and jump on it. Other times I would keep it, and he learned it was my turn to win.

If it was my turn but he really wanted the rope, he wouldn't try to grab it. Instead, he would walk up to me and lick the hand that was holding it. Of course, I would let it go, and that meant so much to him.

We were playing our game one day when he was about 18 months old. As he was running and jumping with the rope, he stopped suddenly and turned and looked right at me.

"Some day I am going to break your heart," he said.

I knew he was right, and what he taught me stays with me to this day. We should enjoy every minute we have with our animals, for they have only one fault: they do not live long enough.

SILENT WORDS

Chapter 3
Comfort & Joy

*This I know, from talking to so many domesticated animals:
They form strong bonds with their human companions and believe it
is their main purpose in life to absorb our emotional hurts, stresses,
and traumas. They do their best to comfort us and relieve our
heartaches and even our everyday tensions.*

The Guide

Labrador Retrievers are among the most favored breeds for
seeing-eye dogs because of their intelligence and sweet dispositions.

Cindy, a black Lab, was being fostered for a guide dogs
program. The foster Mom's job was to socialize Cindy and take her
to obedience classes during the first 18 months of puppyhood. Then
she would be turned over to the organization for training; and if she
passed muster, she would be given to a sight-impaired person.

Cindy's foster Mom, Elaine, had a 14-year-old yellow Lab
named Toby who became the puppy's mentor and in essence raised
her. He was growing more and more dysplastic, but he could get
around well enough to teach her a few things.

When the 18 months were up and it was time to give Cindy
back to the guide dogs organization for training, her foster Mom
swallowed the lump in her throat and did what she had promised to
do.

After a month or two, Elaine received a call. Cindy had acted
up during training and was being kicked out of the program. Would
her foster Mom like to have her?

There wasn't a second of hesitation, and Cindy was soon back
with Elaine. Toby left the physical world five months later.

When I talked to her, Cindy had all kinds of excuses about
"failing" guide dog training.

"They were too fussy and they kept repeating things and I got bored and they wouldn't let me do what I wanted to do and I really wanted to come back here and go swimming in the pool," she said slyly.

Then she revealed the real truth: She knew her Mom would need her when Toby went over to the other side.

Elaine's eyes filled with tears when I told her what the little Lab had disclosed. "I missed Cindy so much when she was gone," she said. "And I don't know what I would have done if she hadn't been here when Toby died. He raised her, so she has some of his personality traits and knowledge."

Cindy knew her Mom would need her, and therefore it was necessary to find a way to come back.

Heart Gap

My parents' small dog moved on to the other side early one morning.

They truly loved this girl of 12 years, and she had gone everywhere with them, even in the camper when they went on vacation.

My Dad would take her on a walk around the block every night, and most of the neighbors would rush out to give Brandy a treat. Everyone loved her, and Dad was especially proud of that fact.

On the morning Brandy left, Dad stepped out onto the front porch to be alone with his thoughts. It was a large veranda that stretched the width of the house, and it was filled with plants.

He noticed a black cat with four white paws hiding behind one of the potted ferns. He was familiar with all the animals in the neighborhood, but he'd never seen this cat before. It watched him, silently, moving its eyes but not its head.

The cat was still there that night, so my parents started feeding him and made him a little bed outside. He seemed to be quite content.

As the days turned into weeks, the cat would greet them in the morning and when they returned in the evening, and he would rub up against them and purr.

He would say, "Pick me up. It will make you feel better."

A few months later my parents decided to get a new puppy, and when they brought her home and introduced her to the cat, the feline was very excited. He kept smelling the puppy and rubbing up against her. He approved of the selection and went to his bed for the night.

The next morning, when Dad went out to feed the cat, he was gone. They never saw him again.

Sometimes they only stay as long as we need them. That little cat was a special soul.

Moves

Janie the Beagle's human companion was a traveling salesman. Ron took her everywhere with him and she loved their life together.

When the time finally came for him to retire, that didn't stop them from traveling. He had a camper, and they took it on fishing trips and went exploring at their leisure.

And then Ron became ill and could no longer sit for long periods of time behind the wheel. He sold the camper because he had no use for it, and he spent most of his time moping around the house. There were no more trips.

Janie became depressed and lost her enthusiasm for life, and that's when Ron called me, because he really loved that little girl.

"I loved going on the moves," Janie told me, "and now we don't go any more."

I explained that the camper was gone, but she countered with, "We could take the other move! (the car)."

That's when I suggested that he take her on short trips to the store, or visiting relatives, or anywhere else that wasn't too far for him to drive. He nodded in agreement, willing to try anything to make her happy again.

"We need to go on moves," Janie added for emphasis. "He needs to get out."

I bumped into Ron a few months later, and he said he was so grateful that Janie had "made" him go on short trips.

"I would have just sat around the house, miserable," he said. "She was really looking out for my best interests."

The Light

Maximilian was a 9-year-old yellow Lab who slowly had been going blind for 3 years, and his Mom wanted to know how much he could still see.

They were inseparable. He went with her everywhere, including to work, and they enjoyed long rides together.

Max wanted her to know that his eyes started feeling better several weeks ago and that he was happy she didn't want another of his kind. He knew he could provide all the comfort and joy she needed.

His Mom also wanted to know why sometimes he would sleep on the bed and other times he wouldn't.

I put the question to him and he showed me a plain white picture, so I decided I needed to go into the bedroom and sit on the floor to see things from his vantage point.

She turned on the overhead light, revealing a white bedspread and white walls. When I got down on the floor and squinted my eyes, there was little separation between the spread and the ceiling. It was all white, just as he had showed me. Because he could only see silhouettes, he couldn't see the edge of the bed, so there was no way he could jump up on it.

I asked her if there was any other lighting she used in the room, and she turned on a lamp next to the bed and turned off the overhead light. I could see the difference immediately.

Max jumped on the bed and lay down on his pillow, contentedly and gently chewing the corner of it as if it were a pacifier, and went right to sleep.

She had adopted him when he was just six weeks old, which is much too young for a puppy to be separated from his mother and littermates. The pillow was, indeed, his pacifier, so when he couldn't jump on the bed, he was missing its comfort as well as the joy of snuggling with Mom.

Sharing

Sandy and her husband are animal lovers, except she is more partial to cats and he prefers dogs.

The dog had passed on and a five-month-old kitten had been added to the household when I went back to visit.

Almost immediately the kitten told me her parents were going to bring home "another animal not my kind." She showed me a silhouette that was obviously an animal, but it was just an outline, blank in the middle. Because Sandy and her husband weren't sure what kind of dog they were getting, they had been thinking about it in vague terms.

I asked them and they confirmed that they had been discussing getting a puppy. They were amused that the kitten had been "reading their minds."

The kitten then flashed me a picture of her little bed sitting off in the corner. "Tell them the new small one not of my kind can have my bed," she said, "because I'm done with it!"

Sandy laughed and verified that the kitten hadn't been near her bed in a month.

It's always fascinating to discover what topics occupy the minds of animals and the capacity they have for making connections.

The puppy will have a cozy bed that smells like his new friend. Comfort and joy, indeed.

Bananas

Ann had a huge draft horse shipped over from Sweden, and, like all good Moms, she wanted to make sure he was comfortable and happy in his new surroundings.

Gandolf told me how different things were in his new home, especially the asphalt on the roads. He was used to dirt tracks and countryside views, but he liked this recent turn of events. He especially was looking forward to his area "getting bigger."

Ann smiled and confirmed that she was planning to expand soon to make sure he had plenty of room.

He then confessed that he missed his sweet yellow things. He was showing me bananas, so I passed that information along to Ann. She said she doubted there were bananas in Sweden, but she vowed to get him some and try them out.

Three months later, Ann called me to come back. She had, indeed, expanded his area, and it contained every comfort a horse could possibly want. It was wonderful. And yes, he loved his bananas!

But he was showing signs of shying away from dogs and getting spooked by things he had previously ignored. After asking him about this, I explained to Ann that once Gandolf became comfortable in his new surroundings, he started seeing more things around him that had gone unnoticed before. They weren't new, but they were new to him. Just like humans, animals go through a period of adjustment when they move, and initially all they see is what is immediately around them.

Finally we discussed what was really bothering Ann. Ever since the expansion, she said, Gandolf would walk away after greeting her when she came home from work. He would lay his head on her shoulder and nuzzle her, and then he would be gone.

His explanation was wonderful. "Now it's time for me to show her my love," he said. "She expanded my area and made it nice, and she did it with love, so I'm showing her that she doesn't have to do anything more for me."

Ann was touched, and I'm quite sure that, despite his best intentions, his disclosure served to bring them even closer together.

Chapter 4
Taste & Distaste

I've discovered that food is as important to animals as it is to us, not just for survival but also for the sweet satisfaction of taste. Domestic animals rely on us for their chow, so we should take their preferences into consideration, as well as their health, and also provide a little variety in the daily fare.

It's All in the Flavor

One winter day, just at dusk, I was at a stable visiting a friend who had purchased a new dressage horse. She really loved this huge dapple gray and wanted to give him everything he liked and to make sure he was as comfortable as possible in his new surroundings.

She wanted to know general things, like was he happy in his new home, what treats and activities he was used to, did he like his new blanket, etc.

About halfway through my conversation with John, he showed me a mental picture of a round, red object and then him dropping it on the ground. The picture was so fast I almost missed it, and I wanted to understand what he was asking me. So I gave John the same picture, except I didn't have him dropping the red object.

He immediately showed himself dropping it on the ground, and a round, green object replaced it in his mouth.

Let me tell you, the taste of bitter green apple was very strong in my own mouth!

I told my friend that John only liked green apples and not to even think about giving him red apples. But she couldn't believe a horse wouldn't want a red apple, so we went to the store and bought a red one and a green one.

Needless to say, John dropped the red one on the ground and contentedly munched the green one. And that was the last red apple my friend ever gave him.

To this day, when I go to visit John, I always make a special stop to get him a green apple.

Cluck!

Jacob was a six-year-old Doberman with a bad stomach condition, and it got to the point where all he would eat was chicken. He loved chicken.

Eventually his illness worsened, and he had to be fed through a tube in his stomach for two months. Again, ground chicken was the preferred meal.

Thankfully, he began to recover, but during his recuperation he would turn his head away when he was offered chicken.

His Mom was perplexed and called me to find out what was wrong.

The explanation was simple, at least in his mind.

"Chicken was only when I was sick," he told me. "Sick is gone; chicken is gone."

We see things one way, but we always have to remember that they frequently see the same situation in an entirely different light.

Not Fast Enough

This was an occasion when I thought for awhile that I'd lost my ability to communicate!

It was a winter night, and a light mist hung in the air around the barn as I talked to my client, Catherine, and her dressage horse, Pure Sport. He was jet black with a perfect white diamond on his forehead. She wanted to make sure he was happy because they had recently changed barns and trainers.

Sport started to become anxious. I needed him to calm down so we could continue our talk, so I asked him to relax.

He said, "I will as soon as I hear the noise and get my red and white thing. I really do not like the noise but I love my red and white thing. Could you tell her to have it ready before she gets here?"

Well, I had absolutely no idea what he was asking for, but I repeated his story to Catherine.

It turned out he was talking about a peppermint candy that needed to be unwrapped before he could eat it. She had no idea the noise from the wrapper bothered him or that it took too long to unwrap it in front of him.

Now she opens his candy before she gets out of the car and has it ready for him by the time she reaches his stall.

It's surprising how things we think are small are really a big deal to our animal companions.

Monkey Business

My client adopted Capp the spider monkey after he retired from the space program. He was a wonderful companion, except for one thing. Whenever she prepared to eat a banana, he would snatch it from her hands and throw it on the ground.

Wanting to get to the cause of this behavior, she called and asked me to come by.

Capp was quite willing to talk. He was worried that the banana would hurt his new Mom. I asked him to explain.

His job had been to test space simulators. He liked having a job because it set him apart from the other simians. He would be strapped into a chair and then whizzed along at a dizzying speed while monitors recorded his heart rate, breathing, etc. Before each test, he would be given a banana to eat.

One day he was supplied with the usual banana, but a technician accidentally hit the start button when the freshly peeled fruit was still in Capp's hand. The resulting explosive speed and G-forces smashed the banana into the startled monkey's face.

From that day forward, he would have nothing to do with bananas, and he had to be given a substitute treat before each test.

"Banana hurt me," he said.

It was as simple as that.

Something's Fishy

Nancy was a nurse, and her long-haired Siamese, Samantha, who was only four years old, had been diagnosed with cancer of the mouth.

31

"It fills with blisters and swells up," Nancy told me, "and then we have to treat it for a week before it goes away. I just want to make sure she's comfortable for as long as possible."

Nancy feared the worst but was trying to cope.

As I talked with Samantha about how she was feeling, she suddenly said, "My mouth doesn't get big all the time."

"When does it get big?" I asked.

"When I get the white box," Samantha answered.

I passed along this information to Nancy, who thought for a moment.

"Every time I go out for a fish dinner," she said, "I bring home the leftovers in a white box! I open the box and cut the fish into pieces for her."

It turned out that Samantha was allergic to the mercury in the fish.

Nancy stopped giving her those tasty morsels, her mouth never swelled again, and she lived to be 18 years old.

It always helps to get a second opinion, especially if it is from the patient!

The Cold Place

A rare liver-spotted Dalmatian was rescued at age five from a dog park, where he'd been abandoned by his owner.

Janet had been looking for a chocolate Lab for some time but hadn't been able to find just the right one. A member of her church told Janet that she'd had a dream in which Janet was near a dog with spots. She didn't think much about it until she got an email from a friend about a Dalmatian that needed a home.

She clicked on the photo and fell in love.

Janet adopted the dog, named him Luther and brought him home to live with her and her mother.

This was a whole new experience for Luther, because he got to spend lots of time in the house. Janet was curious why he spent so *much* of that time lying in front of the refrigerator.

Luther showed me that Janet constantly gave him treats from "the white cold place." So did her Mom. "The good stuff comes from there," he said, and he wanted to be available at all times so he wouldn't miss anything.

Luther had gotten little attention at his previous house, where he'd been kept in the back yard. Now he had a new home and wonderful parents, and all the love and treats were very special to him.

So was the person he called his "living toy." Janet's brother visited frequently and spent all of his time playing with Luther.

I'm sure playtime always ended with a goodie from the white cold place.

SILENT WORDS

Chapter 5
Friendship Matters

Interspecies communication is not that rare, and sometimes friendships develop between the most unexpected partners. Relationships among members of the same species are, of course, very common, and those friendships are often surprisingly sweet.

My Black Things

It was my third appointment of the day and I was feeling good about it, because the owner was an animal trainer. Typically, trained dogs are well behaved and have many exciting things to talk about.

But I was somewhat taken aback by Rex. He was a big German Shepherd, a trained guard dog who would attack on command and protect his property.

As we started to talk, I kept thinking that I hoped the owners would not say the wrong words and give a command by mistake!

Rex's pictures were clear and strong, and he turned out to be a gentle giant. He told me he loved to get the "bad guy" during training so he could show his Mom all he had learned.

Then he said something odd: He would like the house's back door open all the time.

I asked him why.

"Because," he replied, "I can only play with my little black ones outside. But if the door is open, then I can have them inside, too."

"What are his little black ones?" I asked his owner. "He wants them in the house."

She looked down at him and said, "No way, Rex. Your flies are not coming into the house. You'll have to go outside if you want to play with them."

The bigger the soul, the gentler the paw.

Sharing

There are times when we wonder why our animals are no longer doing the things they used to do.

That subject came up with a cat named Kelly, who was one of the most loveable, laid-back felines I've ever met. Whatever you wanted to do was fine with her, and she was very happy in her suburban condo.

Kelly loved her owner, Barbara, and felt very safe with her and her decisions. So, of course, when Mom brought home a kitten, Kelly was right there to meet her new friend.

They started a great relationship, Kelly teaching the kitten what to do and how to stay out of trouble. She was always willing to share food, water, and the biggest thing of all: toys.

Sometimes, although animals communicate with each other all the time, the messages get garbled... much like communication between people. Kelly asked me to intervene and clarify something for the kitten.

"Tell her," she said, "that she doesn't have to try so hard and get frustrated when we race up the stairs. Explain that now her legs are too short and that later she'll be able to keep up with me."

I passed along the message, but I'm not sure the kitten really understood that her legs would grow longer.

One day Barbara called and said, "I have noticed that Kelly doesn't want to sleep with me any more. She sleeps on the chair next to the bed since the kitten came to live with us and started sleeping on the bed. Doesn't she like the kitten? Is she mad at me for bringing home the kitten?

When I asked Kelly about this, she had a wonderful answer.

"No, I'm not mad at her," she said. "I love my new friend and I'm glad she came to live with us. I just wanted them to share some time together so they would get to know each other."

So, if you notice this kind of behavioral change when a new one comes to live with you, thank your animal companions for being so generous with their love.

A Matter of Perspective

I was on my way to see a dog who was experiencing a problem that had come up overnight with her leg, and I was worrying about finding the source of her trouble.

Sometimes what looks like a serious physical ailment to us is not perceived the same way by the animal, so it's difficult to get to the heart of the matter.

When the door opened, two Border Collies stood looking up at me expectantly in the glow of the entry lights. They knew I was there to see them, and we got started right away.

As it turned out, the leg problem was a simple one to pinpoint. Tami, who was an older girl, had twisted her leg jumping off a steep slope in the back yard. When I explained to the owners, Michael and Susan, what had happened, they took immediate steps to fence off the area.

But before I could even think about leaving that night, Tami had a story to tell me.

She said she really loved her companion boy dog, Bo. They were true buddies and did everything together. She sent me a picture of herself, with him as her shadow, and it was apparent they had a great relationship.

Finally, she said, "I love him, but does he have to lick my eyes *all* the time?"

Well, of course I had to pass that question on to the owners. They were very surprised, because they both thought Tami loved having her eyes licked by her friend.

They pledged to work with Bo to keep him from engaging in this activity so often.

About a year later, when Tami was 16, she slipped on the kitchen floor and could not get up. Michael and Susan came home and found her there. They picked her up and discovered she could still walk, then decided – with sorrow in their hearts — to ask me if it was time to set her free.

Tami told me she wasn't prepared to go yet, much to the relief of her parents and Bo. They loved her very much, and this was a reprieve from the inevitable. A month or so later, on Good Friday, Tami was ready to cross over to the other side. She had lived a long and extremely happy life, and her friendship with Bo had kept her young at heart.

Living Brush

It was a hot September morning; and I was visiting a ranch inhabited by many animals, including dogs, horses, cats, and a pot-bellied pig who lived in a dog house.

The pig was the focus of my appointment. "Porker" had grown too large for the house and then too large for the breezeway between structures, where Dad watched sports on TV. Actually, the pig was less interested in the sports than he was the treats that had come his way during the games.

A board that was too tall for Porker to step over had been set up at the end of the breezeway. But it was not so tall that Dad couldn't toss treats over it, and that solution suited the pig just fine. He was quite content, he told me.

I came upon him later, lying down and soaking up the sun's rays. The curious thing was that a calico cat was walking back and forth across his back. I asked the cat what she was doing, and the feline replied that the pig was brushing her fur for her.

"He lies down so I can reach the coarse hairs on his back," she said as she continued to walk over him.

Interspecies friendships always make me smile.

A Gentle Guide

Their names were Laurel and Hardy, and these two beautiful Collies were always together, gamboling around their huge yard. When I met them, Laurel was 5 years old and Hardy was about 18 months.

Hardy was a special-needs dog. He was a little slow mentally and had difficulty making connections between one thing and another, but Laurel was his patient and gentle guide.

I was privy to one conversation between them that really touched my heart, because it showed how sweet and understanding Laurel was and how willing he was to clarify every detail.

Hardy asked Laurel why their parents took them to the park every day, when they already had a park of their own right there at home.

"For the smells," Laurel patiently explained.

Hardy was still confused.

"The away park has different smells than our park," Laurel continued. "Many animals go to the away park and leave their scents. When we go there, we can smell them. And we leave our own scents."

Hardy understood then, but I don't think he really understood how lucky he was to have Laurel for a friend.

The Swimmers

I was visiting with 9-years-young Toy Poodle Kiki to find out how he was getting along with the new rescue dog in the family. He said he needed some alone time away from the constant activities, and he was wishing he still had the swimmers to watch.

"I did the back, and I watched the swimmers," he kept telling me. "And now they're gone.

"Don't tell my Mom I did the back."

I had no idea what he was talking about. As I puzzled over his message, it finally occurred to me that swimmers might be fish in an aquarium. I asked his Mom.

She laughed and said the aquarium had been in the living room high off the floor on a cabinet, next to the sofa. She'd moved it into the hallway onto another cabinet, where Kiki's diminuitive stature prevented him from seeing it.

We had a chuckle over the fact that the little dog had climbed onto the back of the sofa and spent a good deal of time watching the fish swim. Somehow he knew he wasn't supposed to be there, but it had been a relaxing pastime for him that he couldn't resist.

SILENT WORDS

Like any good Mom, she bought some more gold fish and moved the aquarium back onto its cabinet in the living room, where, as far as I know, Kiki is still happily watching his friends from his perch atop the sofa.

Chapter 6
On the Job

Numerous interviews with members of the animal kingdom have taught me that almost all of them feel discomfort if they don't have a job of some kind. Many of these jobs are quite obvious to humans, such as the female lion who hunts for the pride or the Border Collie who herds sheep. Others work in less visible ways, such as the Siamese cat who comforts her owner in times of emotional stress. Dogs, especially, have a deep-seeded need for a job and are happiest when performing their duties.

My Most Challenging Case

Strad was a handsome, fluffy Malamute show dog who was used to being crated and not having much freedom to run.

He was just 13 months old when he came into the possession of a couple who lived on a huge estate. The gated grounds were enormous, both in front of the house and in the back, which included tennis courts and pool.

The only other dog on the premises was an older Golden Retriever who was no longer interested in guard duty. Strad was totally overwhelmed. It was too much ground to cover. When he was guarding the pool, a visitor would appear at the front gate; and if he was on duty in the front, there would be an intruder in the back.

No one asked him to be a guard dog, but he felt instinctively that it was his JOB to protect the estate and his new owners, whom he loved dearly.

Strad's frustration with the situation manifested itself in aggressive behavior toward anyone except his owners. They employed a dog trainer, Bob Penny, who agreed to meet with me so I could help with the case.

My first mission was to gain Strad's trust, but that was no easy task. For the duration of three visits, I sat on the floor inside a sliding glass door while he alternately snarled at me or ignored me from the other side of the glass. Eventually he turned his back on me and laid down, indicating a little acceptance of my presence. We gained some respect for each other that day.

Finally, I suggested that Bob take Strad on a walk outside the property, where they could "accidentally" bump in to me. I thought perhaps the dog would be more relaxed when he wasn't on duty.

I waited down the street. When Bob appeared, I greeted him and ignored Strad. We chatted for some time, not paying any attention to the dog. Eventually he brushed up against my leg and asked to smell my hand. He gave it a good sniff and then announced that I could pet him.

I did, of course, and then he asked to smell my hand again. He explained that he wanted to smell his scent on my hand.

That was the beginning of my long relationship with Strad. I knew the best way to help was to tell him that his Mom and Dad wanted him to guard the back of the premises only when it was light outside and the front only when it was dark. We had quite a conversation about the idea, and he agreed to give it a try.

Breaking down his responsibilities gave him relief from his frustration, and he became much more content over the ensuing weeks. I saw him often, encouraging him and reinforcing the concept.

Once that hurdle was passed, we needed to address the problem of his aggression toward visitors. I brought "guinea pigs" — people who were very familiar with dogs – to the house frequently to interact with him.

It was a group effort, and the entire process took almost a year, but Strad is fine now. He is a happy pooch who still takes his job seriously. His duties just had to be structured correctly and put into the proper context for him.

Useless

Do you ever wonder why dogs chase cats? It might be to spur them into *some* kind of action! I found out early in my career that many dogs feel the way Holly did.

The owner's house had a big back yard with a pool, and I was visiting with Holly, who was of mixed heritage, her Basset friend Cody, and a coal black cat with startling gold eyes.

Holly explained to me that it was her job to guard the yard and the house, and she took her task seriously. Cody was an easy-going little guy who loved everything and everyone. At least he would run to the door to greet people, Holly said, and sometimes he would make the mailman go away; but everything else was her responsibility.

The cat was another matter. She was useless, Holly opined, because she never barked or protected anything. She just hung around and did nothing. Why, the cat didn't even swim!

And that's when I learned that cats don't have jobs like dogs. They usually don't care about having jobs at all, other than giving comfort to their owners.

The Sad Face

My friend the trainer witnessed a woman and an animal control officer both trying to capture the same dog in a park. Animal Control won and took him away, leaving the woman extremely upset. She went to the Pound but was told the dog was going to be destroyed.

The trainer also went to the Pound and argued that the woman, whose name was Melinda, should be allowed to have the animal. He threatened to call the County supervisors and raise a ruckus, and at last Melinda was allowed to take the dog home.

"We had an instant connection at the park," she told me later. "I knew I had to have him."

She called me in for a general consultation and to find out what had happened in the first six months of this German Shepherd-mix's life.

Melinda had named him Gabriel, and he had what can only be described as a very sad expression on his face. But he wasn't sad at all! He told me he was extremely happy to be with her and loved her very much.

"I know my face looks sad," he said, "but I can't help that. It's just my face."

When Gabriel was a little older, Melinda put him in the Delta Society's Pet Partners' training program so he could be an official visitor at hospitals and cheer up the patients.

He readily earned his green vest and I.D. badge at the age of two, but the administrator at the first hospital Melinda tried did not want Gabriel on the premises.

"We prefer to use dogs with Golden Retriever-type personalities," she was told, "and his face is much too sad, anyway."

Melinda took Gabriel to another hospital, where he was accepted, and he now visits mostly elderly patients on a regular basis. He is quiet and well behaved but very loving.

Just to make sure he was enjoying his job, Melinda asked me to find out how he was feeling.

"I love going to visit the people," Gabriel told me. "I know I am making them feel better. I am happy to do my job well."

The expression on his face didn't change, but I knew he wasn't sad at all.

My Blanket

It was a very cold day and raining hard when I went to visit four Labs named Nicky, Sam, Kat and Bob.

Three of the dogs, the owner and I were in the living room when Sam came in carrying a blanket. He laid down on top of it and closed his eyes.

Nicky asked me to come out to his yard so I could see how well he was protecting it. As we walked toward the back of the house, Bob wanted to show me his new food dish table in the kitchen. It was high, which made eating much easier, and he wanted his owner to know how much he liked it.

Again I observed Sam drag his blanket into the room and lay down on it. I was excited about learning the reason for his actions, but he wasn't ready to discuss it yet.

So, off we went to the back yard. We stood under a large patio cover watching Nicky run back and forth, protecting his territory in the heavy rain.

Sam joined us, blanket in tow. "Your blanket is going to get all wet," I said.

He laid down on it and responded: "My blanket stays with me, no matter what."

I asked why.

He told me that when he was a working guy, his previous owner would go into a room and stay there for a long time. Sam learned to take his blanket with him so he'd be close to his owner at all times in case he was needed.

Sam was a seeing-eye dog, and he had loved his job and his sightless friend. But now he was retired, and it was hard for him to let that go.

I told Sam he was a very special guy and that he must have been a great companion.

He looked at me and said he really liked working, but now he was back with the people who had fostered him as a puppy. He loved them for letting him go for a while so he could have an important job.

Feeling useful is vitally important to dogs. Come to think of it, they're not so different from us, are they?

SILENT WORDS

Chapter 7
Land of the Lost

Most of us have experienced the terrible fear of having animal companions disappear, even if it's only for a few hours. They have slipped away somehow, usually just out of curiosity about the world around them. But the important thing for us to realize is that they don't do it to frighten us, and if they are, indeed, lost and alone, they want nothing more than to come back to us.

Fences are Good

Some good friends and clients of mine moved away quite a few years ago and settled in Grant's Pass, Oregon. Their new home had a huge back yard that sloped steeply down to the banks of the Rogue River.

One Spring, on the day after Easter, Deb called me at 6 a.m. She was frantic because their dog, Dixie, had not come home. She had been acquired after they moved, so I had never met Dixie.

Deb emailed me some photos of her and explained that she was elderly and had arthritis. Dixie was a medium-sized mixed breed and much beloved by the family.

I established a mental connection with the dog, and she showed me pictures of her surroundings. Then I described what I saw to Deb.

"There's a huge rock near a bridge," I told her. "Look for that, because Dixie is nearby. It's too hard for her to get up the slope."

She and her husband searched the thick shrubbery along the river but couldn't find their Dixie.

I knew she was there and they were just missing her.

More phone calls ensued.

"Dixie showed me a colored ball just past that rock and a chair," I told them, but they searched all day Monday with no results.

"Don't make me come up there," I joked that night.

"Oh, I would never ask… but would you?" Deb replied, only half in jest.

They searched again all day Tuesday, he walking in the water looking up the river bank, and she walking along a path looking down to the water. Nothing.

On Wednesday morning at 7 a.m., they got a call from neighbors four houses away. They had spotted Dixie struggling up a more gradual slope. She was tired and hungry, but she was alright.

Deb wanted to know where Dixie had made her appearance and went to investigate. Sure enough, a clump of trees hid the rock, the little bridge, the red ball and the chair.

"It was exactly as you described," she told me. "We just couldn't see it."

I was greatly relieved to hear the news. There's nothing worse than losing an animal.

And, to prevent further escapades of this nature, my friends wisely decided to put up a fence.

He Was Only "Lost" to Her

When my phone rings at 6 a.m., I know there's an emergency. At least my friends and clients let me sleep until dawn, even though they've probably been up all night worrying about whatever has happened.

On this particular morning, Cindy was frantic. She lives in the mountains with 10 cats, 4 dogs, a horse, a 3-year-old daughter named Holland, and a husband.

"I've looked everywhere," she exclaimed, "and I can't find Tigger! I even looked all around the outside of the house."

The cats, I knew, preferred to stay indoors.

"Relax," I told her. "He's in the house. He says he had an argument with Peanut and wants to be left alone."

"But Holland and I have searched every room," she protested, "and we can't find him anywhere. And now I have to take Holland to day camp."

"Look again," I suggested. "He's showing me the big room."

Several more phone calls ensued while her daughter was at camp. Cindy also called her husband, who works many miles away, and begged him to come home and help her look. Most people reject logic when they are upset, and Cindy was no exception. She really wasn't listening to what I was saying.

"You have to find Tigger before Holland comes home," I told her. "Stop wasting your time outside and in the other parts of your house. He's in the family room."

The final phone call in this episode was quite amusing.

"I was standing in the kitchen," she said, "wondering what to do, when Tigger casually strolled up the stairs from the family room. He drank some water, ate a bite of food, and just as casually sauntered back down the stairs."

I chuckled to myself.

"I recovered from the shock in time to follow him," she continued, "and then watched as he climbed back into his hidey-hole in the family room. He was BEHIND a drawer that wasn't quite shut!" So Tigger wasn't really lost at all. He knew exactly where he was: safe at home. Sometimes they just don't want to be found.

Back to School

George the Basset, his buddy, Beau, and their family had just moved to a new home, and the two friends decided to explore the neighborhood that Friday afternoon. They escaped through a back gate and disappeared. Beau came home that evening, but George was nowhere to be found.

The family called me Saturday. I said George was showing me a house on a corner that was being remodeled. It had a chain link fence around it, and George had squeezed under it and spent Friday night there. Then he showed me what appeared to be an elementary school.

A week went by and I heard nothing. The following Saturday I got a call: George had been home since Monday, and the family wanted me to come over and ask him where he had been. I was happy to hear the little guy was OK.

"Every time I tried to come home I ran into a circle," George explained. The streets in that neighborhood, I had noticed, curved around off of other streets, so it was quite confusing, especially to a little fellow who was so low to the ground.

Beau, who was bigger and taller, got separated from his buddy but was able to find his way home.

"I missed licking his ears when he wasn't here," Beau interjected, obviously happy his friend had returned.

George went on with his story. He had spent the night at the house with the fence and then moved on to the schoolyard Saturday. On Sunday, by now tired and very hungry, he was trotting down an unfamiliar street when some nice people stopped, picked him up and took him home for the night.

It was the family's turn to continue the saga. The people who sheltered George had called the Pound to say they had found a Basset. When the family checked with the Pound on Monday morning, the message was there.

George was four miles away. As they drove to pick him up, they saw the house on the corner with the chain link fence and they also passed the schoolyard.

I don't think George will want to go exploring again; but just in case he gets the urge, he now has a microchip and the back gate is permanently locked.

The Search for Carson

I was invited to have a consultation booth at the National Golden Retriever Specialty, which was held in Southern California's beautiful Malibu hills. It was October and extremely warm, and the sea breezes weren't reaching us, even though we were only six miles from the ocean.

But the Calamigos Ranch setting was perfect for the four-day show. Agility, obedience, and conformation rings were set up between huge trees of every description that provided shade around rolling expanses of grass. The Los Angeles club hosting the event had used a "Hollywood Gold" theme that was carried out to the smallest detail, and there was an air of festivity everywhere I looked.

I remember it all as if it were yesterday, and I remember Trish. She came to my booth looking a little skeptical, and the first thing she asked was if I knew Bea Lydecker. I explained that Bea had been my mentor, and Trish told me she had spent time with her back in the 1970s when Bea was working with the Sacramento Police Department and Trish was a community volunteer there.

It was a pleasant surprise to meet someone who knew Bea, and we hit it off right away. But I didn't expect to hear from Trish again so soon because she lived in Northern California.

Right after Christmas, I received a long distance call, and the frantic woman on the line was Trish. A friend's much beloved Golden, 14-year-old Carson, had been dog-napped.

She explained that her friend had left Carson in a van overnight, sitting in her daughter's driveway in what was considered to be a very safe neighborhood. In the morning there was nothing left in the driveway but broken glass.

Trish and others from the local Golden club had contacted the police and had been searching everywhere for the van and the dog. Carson's Mom was understandably distraught and they all were desperate for some guidance.

I took a moment and established a connection with Carson. He was no longer with the van or the man who stole it, I told Trish. He was safe and he was not afraid. Where he'd gotten out of the van, there was a large, bright, lighted sign, a mini-mall and a gas station. And there was a street nearby named after a tree or flower. I also told Trish that they needed to get lost dog signs out right away and that I felt confident they would find him.

I had to leave my house then, so I explained I would be unreachable for several hours. It was days before I heard what had happened.

Trish and her friends spread out, looking for areas that matched what I had described, but there was no sign of Carson. In one of the mini-marts Trish visited, she met a sympathetic woman who offered to take the information and call if she heard anything.

Exhausted, the friends regrouped at the scene of the crime and decided to call Bea in Oregon, since I was unavailable. Bea said that Carson had been lying down in the back of the van, uncrated, when it was stolen. After a period of time that could have been anywhere from five to twenty minutes, he stood up and walked to the front of the van, placing his head near the driver's shoulder. In shock, the man had swerved the van sharply to the side of the road, jumped out, and opened the door so Carson could exit the vehicle. According to Bea, if Carson hadn't gotten out, the man was so frightened he was ready to abandon the van.

Bea also said she saw Carson walking in a drainage ditch and there was a strong smell of cows. Unfortunately, in that part of California, there are farms and cows everywhere. Nevertheless, the friends continued their search far and wide until it was almost dark.

Trish finally returned to the house where Carson was stolen and discovered that her friend's daughter had just received a call from someone who'd found a dog matching his description. He'd been wandering on the front lawn at 6 a.m. and the family had put up "found dog" signs all over the neighborhood. The woman Trish had spoken to at the mini-mart had made the connection!

Naturally, Trish went along to the home where Carson was purported to be. At the street's corner, there was the large, bright, lighted sign and cluster of small businesses I had described, and nearby was a street named Walnut. The scent of cows was in the air and a drainage ditch ran by the side of the road. And Carson was, indeed, safe and unafraid.

It's amazing that, after years of little contact, Bea and I were able to work a case "together," even though we were in different states.

Shergar

Perhaps my most famous "lost" animal case took place in the early 1980s, when authorities twice flew me to northern Ireland to help search for Shergar.

He was a famous racehorse who, I was told, had won the 1981 Derby by a record 10 lengths. Shergar was then 5 years old, and about to begin his second year at stud, when he disappeared. He belonged to the Aga Khan and a syndicate of other owners.

It was surmised that Shergar had been taken by the IRA for ransom. I was called in several weeks after his disappearance, and the trail was truly cold. Nothing came to me... not a picture, not a presence, not a feeling... nothing. I have since learned that usually means the animal is dead. Nevertheless, I was flown back again for another try, but the result was the same. Nothing.

Twenty-five years later, London's Sunday Telegraph re-opened the case and interviewed many of the previously close-mouthed individuals who knew different parts of the story. It seems Shergar was indeed kidnapped by the IRA for ransom, but the syndicate balked at paying, fearing that would lead to additional horse-nabbings. The animal then became a liability, and on day 4 he was, tragically, machine-gunned to death and buried in a remote part of the country.

I was saddened to read this account, because no animal deserves to die that way, and because I was summoned too late to find him alive.

Fonzie's Detour

When Rick called me, I could hear the pain and desperation in his voice. His dog Fonzie had been missing for 8 days, and the ordeal was making Rick physically ill.

Fonzie had gone out for his usual 15-minute pre-bedtime run and had never returned. Rick had called the shelters, looked for him at "their" park, and checked the parking lot at work. No one had seen the Fonz.

Rick's Mom arrived to help, and they put up lost dog flyers everywhere. Still nothing. He was so afraid his best friend had been hit by a car and was lying somewhere by the side of the road.

I told him Fonzie was still alive and on his way home, and that all he wanted was to get back to Rick and tell him how sorry he was and that he would never stray again.

I'm not sure Rick was convinced. But Fonzie reappeared the next night, mysteriously tied to the porch post. They were elated to see each other again, but Fonz was in bad shape physically and Rick wanted to know what had happened to him.

When I arrived at their apartment, the two of them were sitting close together, and Fonzie began sending me his telepathic pictures.

For a reason he didn't really understand, Fonzie had taken a detour that night from his usual trek to a nearby school, and then he'd become lost and confused. Eventually he ended up at their park, where he met a stray dog who told him about a woman who fed homeless animals. They stayed near her for a couple of days, and then Fonzie went back to his search for a way home.

He was lost for several days among the maze of residential streets, and even crossed the freeway, barely avoiding being hit by a car. He was frightened, confused, and hungry. Fonzie finally came upon a small grocery store, where a man and two boys tied a rope around his neck and put him in their pickup truck. They took him home and kept him tied up in the back yard for 4 days.

Fonzie shook off his depression and waited for an opportunity to escape, which was provided when one of the boys left a gate open. He bolted and eventually made his way to the park. From there he remembered the alley that led to Rick's apartment, and was halfway there when a rope fell over his head and tightened around his neck. Frustrated, he walked along with his captor. And then he began to sense that he was drawing closer to Rick. The stranger, who was actually one of Rick's neighbors who had seen the flyers, tied Fonzie to the porch post and left him there. He couldn't reach the door to scratch, so he just whined and whined until Rick's Mom heard him and opened the door.

Rick had been asleep on the couch, and he awoke to the feel of Fonzie's head on his neck and the sound of his soft whimpers. The nightmare was over.

Chapter 8
A Failure to Communicate

As you might well imagine, there is ample opportunity for miscommunication and misunderstandings between animals and their humans. We just don't look at the world the same way, and, of course, there is the "language" barrier.

Ears Do More Than Hear

I hate to be late for an appointment, but there I was stuck in traffic, stewing about making my newest client wait.

As it turned out, I got to the condo in time to meet Buddy, a five-year-old, small mix dog with very short legs.

He immediately told me he wanted to "win sometimes." When I inquired about what that meant, he explained that they all ran up the stairs at night, and he wanted to finish the "race" first at least once in a while. I passed along this sentiment to his amused Mom and Dad.

Buddy then wanted to know if his owners still loved his ears, so I asked them what he could possibly mean by that.

They looked confused and surprised by the question, as is often the case.

"Of course we love his ears," Dad said. "We think they're great. Why is he asking that?"

"He says you used to rub them all the time," I replied, "but now you've stopped doing it."

Mom started to laugh. "About two years ago," she said, "the little guy had a condition that required medication to be put on the tips of his ears three times a day. Of course, when they were healed, we stopped rubbing them."

Now his ears are caressed daily, just to show him they love him. It's important to remember that sometimes our smallest acts are significant to our animal companions.

Grass is Green

I received a call about a seven-year-old Golden Retriever who had started to wet in the house.

When I arrived, I noticed that the house had been completely renovated and redecorated and looked quite different than it had on my previous visits.

I settled into a chair and asked Missy why, after all the years going outside, she was now going inside.

She looked up at me and said, "I only go on my grass."

"Yes, but they tell me you are going inside the house now."

"I only go on my grass," she said again. "Now I have an inside grass and an outside grass. They only want me to go on my grass."

I revealed to her owners what she had said, but they had no clue what she was talking about. So, I asked her to show me the inside grass.

She took me to the brand new den in the back of the house, and there it was: green, wall-to-wall carpeting.

I broke the news to her owners, who were amazed that their dog associated grass with the color green.

The carpet color has since been changed, and now she only has her outside grass, which she uses with pride.

A Bed is Not Just a Bed

Sometimes a dog's bed is her castle. At least that's the way Amy felt about hers. A large mixed breed, she and her owner, Marie, truly loved each other; but as is often the case in even the closest relationship, there was a misunderstanding.

We were having a great discussion when Amy started talking about her bed. She wanted to know why her bed moved but her owner's never did.

With a smile on her face, Marie explained that she moved Amy's bed downstairs every morning so the dog would have a place to sleep while the owner worked. At night she would take it back upstairs so Amy could sleep in the same room with her.

"Well," I suggested, "you need to do something different with the bed situation. Maybe you could get another bed, so there'd be one upstairs and one downstairs, instead of moving one from place to place."

Amy got a second bed that very day. Now her castle is always wherever she is, and it never gets moved.

You see, Amy was a rescued stray who had previously suffered abuse, and this was her very first bed. She took it seriously.

The Deal

Fancy was a beautiful black racehorse who did very well in the morning workouts but never won any of her races, which were in the afternoon. Horses like that are called "Morning Glories."

Her owners wanted to know why, so Fancy and I had a conversation at the ranch where she lived.

"Are you nervous about the starting gate?" I asked her.

"No."

"Is it too hot in the afternoon?"

"No."

"Is it the condition of the track?"

"No."

"Then why do you fall back during the races?"

"Because they like me," she said.

I asked her to explain.

"When I don't win," she answered, "then we're all there together in the barn. I get to stay with the other horses."

Fancy was trailered to the race tracks from her ranch. When she lost, which she always did, the trainer would insist that she stay for a week so he could work with her some more.

I decided to make a deal with her by switching the outcomes.

"If you win," I said, "then you'll get to stay with the other horses. But if you lose, then you'll have to go home."

She didn't quite believe me 100 percent, so in her next race she came in second.

"Well, I guess you're going home," I told her.

"If I stay this time," she said, "then there won't be any more horses in front of me. I'll put them all behind me."

I agreed to give her one more chance, and she won her next race and continued to win. Needless to say, it changed her life.

Angel?

A friend of mine, who is a dog obedience trainer, had been working with a female German Shepherd named Fay. She was doing very well and he felt that his job was complete. But the owner was having problems keeping Fay under control when they went on walks, so Mom kept calling the trainer to come back and work with the dog some more.

My friend wanted to get to the bottom of the problem, so he asked me to meet him when he next visited Fay and her owner.

I got to the house a little early on that cool fall afternoon, so that I could see what was going on before the trainer arrived. Fay, Mom and I took off on a walk among the scattered leaves, and sure enough, the dog was out of control. But the owner was yelling, screaming and carrying on worse than the dog.

When the trainer got there, Fay ran over to him and said, "Why are you here? Am I not an angel?"

You see, the trainer had always told her that she walked like an angel. But the owner always spoke loudly and *never* told her she walked like an angel. Fay was confused!

A dog matches the energy level of the person with him/her, and in this case the situation escalated as the owner got more and more excited when Fay didn't "behave."

Mom needed to be more patient and speak softly. Once I explained that to her and she acted on it, Fay became her "Angel" too.

Pick Me Up

Mary Ann, a four-year-old yellow lab, suddenly quit walking. Her parents took her to vets and specialists from one end of the state to the other, trying to find out what was wrong.

They finally called me on someone's recommendation. It was one of my very first cases, and I was worried because the situation seemed to be serious.

Mary Ann had a special area in the garage and was lying on her special bed. She wasn't indicating that anything was bothering her physically, and I could feel no heat – a sure sign of discomfort — emanating from her body. I began to question her, but her answers were monosyllabic and she wasn't elaborating on anything.

"Two little ones upstairs," she finally said. "It's their fault."

I was beginning to fear that this session would not be successful, or, at the very least, it was going to take hours to understand the situation.

Eventually, with gentle prodding from me, she was more forthcoming and showed me lots of people coming in and out of the house, continuously picking up little dogs and putting them down. She was being ignored.

I had no idea what any of this meant, so I consulted with the owners. It turned out that the two little black dogs had had a litter of ten puppies, so there had been a flow of people coming to see them and trying to decide which ones to take home.

Downstairs again with Mary Ann, I explained that the puppies were gone.

"If I stop walking, they will pick me up, too," she said, elaborating on her state of mind.

It all became clear. Once her parents understood, it only took a couple of days and lots of attention to get Mary Ann back on her feet.

The Noise

After his Dad died, a cute little Yorkie named Max came to live with his friend Teddy and Teddy's Dad, Jim.

Max had witnessed his parent's death – drowning in a bathtub – but Teddy and his owner were familiar to him and, although he was sad, this was the next best place to live.

Jim called me to make sure the new living arrangements were OK with both dogs.

"It's OK for Max to stay," said Teddy the Cocker mix, "but when I get busy, he needs to do something else."

Getting busy, it turned out, meant lying on the upstairs balcony and watching birds!

Jim told me that every few days Max would walk away from his food bowl and refuse to eat, and Jim was concerned.

When I asked Max about that, he said, "But it was my time to make the noise. I never get to make the noise anymore. He put the noise on the floor for me, and when I make the noise, then I get to eat."

I told Jim what he'd said, and, although it made no sense to me, the man began to smile.

It seems that Max' former owner would put the electric can opener on the floor every third day or so at dinner time, as a treat. Max would touch it and it would make the noise, and that was his job.

Needless to say, his new Dad started the same routine.

The Skeptic

As I pulled up in front of the *cul de sac* address, a man stepped out of the house to greet me and escorted me inside. Jim introduced himself, explained that his wife would appear shortly, and then left me standing in the middle of the living room. He actually went outside and disappeared.

His wife and her mother eventually came downstairs and were surprised that Jim had left me alone, but their charming little black Lab had been entertaining me. Her name was K'lee.

We chitchatted about this and that, and finally we heard Jim come back into the house. His wife corralled him and made him sit in the living room. It was obvious that he was somewhat skeptical.

"Tell my Dad thank you for rescuing me twice," K'lee said.

That got Jim's attention. "She was a rescue," he revealed, "and then she escaped and I went looking for her and brought her home again."

K'lee sent me more pictures: "I came to them when they really needed me."

Jim was looking more and more thoughtful. "So how long did it take you to investigate us and find out all these things?" he said. Then he laughed.

K'lee told me she really missed her "big water bowl," and when I disclosed that information, Jim's remaining suspicions melted away.

"OK, you couldn't have known that," he exclaimed, "because there's no evidence it was ever there!"

Jim explained that there had been a fish pond in the back yard, and the Lab was always getting wet, so he had filled in the pond and planted grass over it.

He then invited me into the back yard and enthusiastically asked me where K'lee would like him to put the NEW fish pond. It was obvious that he loved this little girl and wanted to make her happy, and that made me happy.

Sometimes skeptics become the most energetic believers.

Months later, I received a message that K'lee was acting up, and Jim and his wife thought it might be some kind of separation anxiety. I went to visit.

"My friend isn't here anymore," K'lee announced when I was barely inside the door.

"Before the wets came, lots of things happened. My Mom was here all the time, and now she's not here all the time. And my Dad took me on many moves. And when I bark I get to go in the big water bowl. And I like the boy who walks with me, but my Dad doesn't walk with me as much, so I can't help him. And I get confused and sad and one time I went in my den."

It was obvious there had been some upheaval in that household, so I began to translate K'lee's video to her Mom and Dad.

Jim explained that his wife's Mom (the "friend") was no longer living there and had left before the big rains came to So. California. Then his wife was hospitalized, was home on medical leave for awhile, and now she had gone back to work. Jim's son had suffered a heart attack, so he had taken K'lee on trips to visit him. With all that was happening, Jim hadn't had time to walk her as much as usual, so the boy across the street had taken over that duty. The boy's mother would hear K'lee barking in frustration and would come and get her and let her swim in their pool. And yes, K'lee had had an "accident" in Jim's house.

Domesticated animals take great comfort in routine, I explained, and when that routine is disrupted they become anxious. So K'lee's behavior under the circumstances was perfectly understandable. Although things were getting back to normal, Jim still wasn't walking her in the evenings, and that was upsetting her the most.

You see, providing comfort to Jim was K'lee's *job*, and he was no longer giving her the opportunity to help him.

Now that he understood, he promised he would return to the evening walk and spend more quality time with his little girl. And no doubt the skeptic has discovered that she's very good at her job.

Misdiagnosis

A friend and client had moved to another part of the state and acquired a new dog named Dixie.

When Dixie was still quite young, Deb called to tell me that her girl had been diagnosed with something that was killing her white blood cells. The recommendation was euthanasia.

Dixie told me she was fine and didn't understand her Mom's concern, and I suggested to Deb that she get a second and even third opinion. She did, and by the time she got to the third vet, Dixie could not sit up.

Heartbroken, Deb drove to a park and carried Dixie to a nice spot under a tree, where they cuddled and had a long talk. Then Deb called me again.

As she had before, Dixie told me she was fine and most certainly was not ready to leave her Mom. I told Deb to try another vet.

Veterinarian number 4 diagnosed heartworm, and Dixie recovered completely. That was many years ago and she is still with her Mom.

It's always a good idea to get the patient's take on the situation!

For example, a client's horse was limping, but the vet could find nothing wrong with his back left leg. When I was called in to consult, the patient showed me what had happened.

"After the last wet time," he said, he had been walking on brick; and as he rounded the corner of a building, his back right leg had slipped and his front left shoulder had hit a protruding bar.

The owner and the vet had been looking for the source of the injury in the wrong place.

Snakes!

An All-American dog I know once said, "Tell my Dad I like the long moves (car rides) and the walk better than the short move and the walk. The short move is only to the green area (park), and it only has smells of my kind."

Dad explained that he had a mountain cabin, but he was always nervous about his dog being bitten by a snake. He wanted me to tell his companion to stay away from them.

When I showed the dog a picture of a snake, he said, "I see the little ones at home and the big ones after the long moves." He thought snakes were just a larger version of worms!

"You need to stay away from the big ones," I told him, but he wanted to know why. I did my best to explain about bites and venom, and finally he understood.

Now he gets to go on many more long car rides and walks with his Dad, and he especially loves the variety of smells. There's one smell, however, that he avoids.

Long Distances

The beginning of this story is more about long distance communication than lack of communication. We'll get to the miscommunication later.

A friend had acquired a thoroughbred horse in Europe and needed to bring her to California. The trip required her to travel by boat and then plane, and he was worried she would be afraid.

I contacted her and explained that she would be on something big and soft and then she would go up. I told her she would be OK, and I stayed in touch on and off during her long journey.

When we met her at the airport, she said to me, "I know who you are." That made me smile.

She was young and green and needed to learn how to carry a rider, so her owner sent her to stay with a highly recommended horse trainer for four months. Unfortunately, when she returned, only her spirit had been broken. The cowboy had used conventional methods of force and intimidation; and instead of making her fit to ride, he had made her skittish and fearful. She was not a happy girl.

Dismayed, and desperate to reverse the process, the owner sent her to a place closer to home that specialized in the Pirelli method of horse training. This involves a gentle touch and a gentle voice and winning the horse's trust a little at a time. I'm pleased to report that it worked! My friend now has an equine companion who is more than happy to provide "transportation."

Leave the Cold On

A rambunctious, 3-year-old black Lab named Jake made my day with the issues he wished to discuss.

His Mom and I were greatly amused when he said, "Tell my Mom she can leave the cold on all she wants. I love it." We'd had a warm spell in the middle of winter, and Jake preferred cool weather. He expected her to control the conditions outside just as she controlled the temperature inside the house.

I laughed and explained to him that this was not possible. Although disappointed, Jake was undeterred in his quest to have all issues addressed.

He was concerned that there might be additions to the family and wanted to be reassured. "No others of my kind and no small furs" he said adamantly, meaning no other dogs or cats. I passed along the message with a grin.

He changed the subject. "My away toy isn't here anymore when I need to play with him," Jake complained. His Mom's son had become a medical intern and was on duty 24 hours every other day. I did my best to explain that the away toy could not be with him as often as he used to be.

Domesticated pets often put humans into simple categories. Mom and/or Dad are the people who feed them and rule their worlds, while other members of the family, or frequent visitors who play with them, are considered toys. It's good to know your place.

SILENT WORDS

Chapter 9
Rescue Me

Some of the most poignant stories come from animals who have been rescued by caring people devoted to improving the lives of these often unfortunate creatures. A new home means comfort and lots of love, but sometimes previous experiences affect the animal's attitude and behavior.

The Sheet

Larry came into Margot's life at the age of five after she adopted him from a Lake Los Angeles rescue group. He was a big black Lab and he arrived with a bed sheet in tow.

He promptly buried the sheet in the back yard, and almost every night thereafter, he would dig it up and bury it elsewhere. If towels were left unattended, he would bury them, too.

After six years of loving this beautiful dog and trying to overlook his odd behavior, Margot heard about me from a friend and gave me a call.

Larry was reluctant to get too close to me (or anyone other than Margot) at first, so of course I respected his space. I sat on the floor and asked him about the sheet, bracing myself emotionally for what was to come.

He told me he moved the sheet so they couldn't be found and he wouldn't have to hear their cries. I asked him to explain.

When he was two or three months old, he lived with two other puppies. They were beaten to death and buried in a sheet in the back yard. He was also beaten, but kept alive, and he suffered at the hands of these individuals for five years.

I have learned to hold back my anger and pain, because to disclose it to an animal might cause him or her to misunderstand the meaning of my emotions. It took all of my will power to clear my mind and remain calm that day.

I'd brought a new sheet with me, and I cut it in half. I told Larry that both halves were his to do with as he wished and suggested that he leave one on his bed. He did, and then he buried the other. I told him that the sounds were gone and that he would always be safe in his new yard. He could leave the buried sheet where it was.

As I knelt next to the spot where the half-sheet was buried, reassuring him that his Mom now understood the situation, Larry gently touched his nose to my shoulder. That touch went straight to my heart.

In the year that followed, Margot reinforced every day the notion that his yard was safe and that the sounds were gone, and Larry sometimes left the sheet in one place for as long as a week.

He crossed over to the other side at the age of 12, knowing that he was deeply loved, but never quite forgetting the frightful beginning of his life.

Larry's companion, Cinnamon, was lonely after he left the physical world, so of course Margot adopted another rescue dog to share her heart and her home.

And every day I am thankful that people like Margot exist.

Walking the Pan

Betty had rescued a young Beagle mix from the Pound and named him Jack. She caught him just in time, as he was about to be euthanized for aggressive behavior.

There had been an instant connection between them, and she had insisted on taking him home against the advice of his keepers.

She wanted to make sure he was happy and comfortable, so she called me to find out what he had to say.

"Tell her she saved my life!" Jack said enthusiastically as soon as I arrived. "I am so grateful to her! And tell her how much I love walking the pan."

I passed on the information and asked a smiling Betty what he meant by "walking the pan."

Jack had been a street dog, she explained, and the pads of his paws were torn from the asphalt. Every day she would fill a long, shallow pan with warm salt water and then walk him back and forth through it to help heal his wounds.

It was a comforting and very special time for him each day.

When I revealed to her how much this ritual meant to Jack, Betty vowed to continue the practice even after his paws had healed. They just wouldn't need the salt.

It's always surprising to discover how much the little things mean to our animal companions.

No Time to Cover

Mary found a 12-month-old tabby cat on the street and named her Megan. She brought the kitty home and introduced her to the elderly cat Patrick, who promptly took her under his paw and showed her how to live in a house.

All was well, except Megan would never "cover" in the cat box, no matter how much Mary and Patrick encouraged her.

I visited and asked Megan why she didn't do what was an instinctive motion for all felines.

"When I was out on the street I was small and frightened," she explained, "and I never had time to cover. I had to keep moving!"

I told her she was safe now and could take all the time she wanted.

Three days later, Mary was awakened in the middle of the night by the sound of scratching, and scratching… and scratching.

Megan was in the litter box, apparently overcompensating for her previous lapses in feline etiquette!

Several months passed, and then her old friend Patrick crossed over. She missed him, but when a new kitty came to live with her and Mary, Megan was prepared to become the mentor. And the first thing she taught it was how to use the litter box!

(This story continues in "Reunited at Last.")

Filling the Void

Paula lost her Airedale, Ben, on Saturday night, setting him free with the help of her compassionate veterinarian. That's when she heard about Dixie, a 10-pound, 17-years-young Poodle for whom the vet was trying to find a home.

Dixie was a sweetheart, so Paula took her; and when she went to register her with Animal Control, she heard about CeeCee. The black Cockapoo was 13, and her owner, an elderly woman, had passed on.

Paula told the Animal Control Officer that she wanted CeeCee and that she'd come back for her that evening. The dog was scheduled for euthanasia the next day because no one had adopted her.

The Animal Control Officer put a big "Adopted, do not kill" sign on CeeCee's cage, but when he went back to check on her later that day, the crate was empty. He ran all the way to the euthanasia room and scooped her off the table – just in time!

When Paula and I arrived, we approached the kennel and observed the fluffy black mop. Only CeeCee's eyes moved as she looked up at us.

I asked if she'd like to come and live with Paula and Dixie. She missed her human companion, the dog said, but her final comment was this:

"I'll give it a try."

So Paula took CeeCee home to join Dixie. It wasn't long before the Poodle and the Cockapoo were looking up at Paula with love in their hearts and smiles on their faces.

"Love never stops," Dixie told me. "It just moves from one soul to another."

A year later, Paula adopted an Airedale puppy, and CeeCee passed on almost immediately.

Dixie stayed for another year and a half.

They had all filled a void in each other's lives, even though it was only for a short time. Such is the value of adopting a rescued animal.

A Thank You Gift

Tony was a pure black cat who seemed to dislike all people except his owner. He would run into the closet and hide if anyone else appeared.

His Mom had rescued him from the Pound, and he lived with another kitty who was quite people-friendly.

Whenever Mom had to go out of town on business, her mother would come over and cat-sit her "grandchildren."

Grandma wanted to know why Tony always put a mouse toy in his water bowl.

From his perch in the closet, Tony told me he hid because he was afraid someone would take him away from his Mom.

I assured him that I had no intention of taking him anywhere, and then I asked about the mouse toy in the water bowl.

"I can't bring the outside in," he replied, "so I give her one of my toys to thank her for taking care of me."

What a sweet little boy he was! I advised Grandma to tell Tony "Thank you" and then take the toy home with her. She could return it at a later date when he wasn't looking.

Her Throw Rug

Grandmother's dog Misty came to live with two girls and their Mom after the elderly woman passed on.

The little golden-colored "house slipper" was six or seven years young, and all was well in her new home.

There was just one problem: Misty kept wetting on the bathroom rug.

When I asked her about it, she said, "Only for me. My rug."

Further conversation revealed that Misty had been trained to go on a small throw rug just inside the back door of her former owner's house. Grandmother had been arthritic, and she couldn't always get to the door to let Misty out. She just kept buying a new rug.

"I remember that rug!" her granddaughter said. "One was always there, only sometimes it was a different color."

The bathroom mat was the only throw rug in Misty's new home, so naturally she thought that's where she was supposed to go.

To change her behavior, her new family put in a doggie door and also bought a small mat to be placed inside the back door. Gradually, the rug was moved outside and the problem was solved.

When we adopt an animal, we must try to be understanding of behavior that seems odd to us. There's always a good reason!

My Treasures

Janet adopted Bogie and Maddie from the Pound after her beloved Misty crossed over to the other side following a struggle with Diabetes and other ailments. But I'd never met Janet before and didn't know about Misty.

Maddie was a calm, loving young tabby, but the jet black kitten was a handful. Bogie would streak around the house, climbing on shutters and hiding in closets. He would not let Janet pick him up.

When I was invited to find a cause for this behavior, I saw him for just a brief moment as he scampered through the room. Luckily, I don't need eye contact to communicate with an animal.

Before I could explore his aversion to being picked up, Bogie gave me a puzzle. "The noise takes my treasures away," he said, showing me some huge leaves.

Janet thought about that for a minute and decided that the noise must be the gardener with his leaf blower.

Bogie explained further. As an indoor kitty, he loved to look out the sliding glass doors and observe the pointy leaves decorating the patio, because his little lizard friends would hide under them. When the noise came, his treasures would blow away and the lizards would scurry for cover.

It's always fascinating to learn what animals treasure, and it's equally fascinating to learn what they like to avoid, and why.

I finally got Bogie to discuss his behavior. "I don't like ups," he said. "No ups, because ups hurt me before." Being picked up made him feel like he was going to fall. You see, he had been dropped when he was a tiny kitten.

When I explained this to Janet, she immediately decided to respect his feelings and be content with petting him. What a good Mom! And Bogie loved her for it.

There was a bonus to this session. I kept feeling a presence behind me and eventually told Janet there was another being in the room who had a message for her. I asked if she'd had a previous cat, and she said yes.

"He says he's OK and what happened wasn't your fault," I said, "and it's time to move on. And he's also asking me to tell you that he still loves his tuna."

Janet, who is a cheerful and positive person, burst into tears. "Tuna was his favorite treat," she cried. "That hit home."

Despite the tears it caused initially, the visit from Misty was Janet's reward for being such a great Mom.

Noise

Beau and Fritz live in a wonderful home with a backyard that resembles a beautiful park: expanses of grass, trees, and a pool. They have kind, loving parents and get the best of care and lots of attention.

And they deserve every bit of it, because such was not always the case.

A friend found the pups after Laurie had lost her two elderly dogs – Oscar and Felix — within a month of each other.

Beau and Fritz had been living on the streets and had been rescued by a kindly woman who wanted to locate a good home for both of them. Laurie's friend found out about them and put the two parties together.

The dogs were young, and the bigger one – Beau – was skittish and overly protective of Fritz. Laurie thought perhaps they were father and son. Even though they didn't look alike, there were some similarities. Beau was mostly yellow Lab and Fritz resembled a fox, yet both had spotted tongues and big black rings around their eyes.

From the beginning, they were gentle and well behaved but fearful of almost everything. They had no interest in toys. Loud voices frightened them and they disappeared when visitors arrived. They were afraid of the ceiling fans.

But Laurie and her husband were up to the task, and their kindness, love and understanding made the boys very happy and comfortable.

Five years had passed when I first met Beau, Fritz and Laurie. The dogs still didn't play with toys, and Beau was still uneasy about visitors' loud voices and other noises, but otherwise all was fine.

I sat down on the floor to talk to them, and Beau took the lead. He and Fritz were brothers from different litters. When they were young, they and their mother were driven up into the foothills, pushed out of the car, and left behind to survive on their own.

At some point in time, Beau was standing next to his mother when he heard a loud noise. His mother fell over and was dead.

From the pictures he gave me, I have to assume she was shot. In any case, Beau was very frightened. Fritz was just a little puppy, so Beau quickly told him to follow and they ran away. They managed to survive for several months before the kindly woman coaxed them into trusting her.

To this day, when Beau hears a loud noise, he's afraid he will fall over. He has acute hearing, so any noise out of the ordinary disturbs him.

I told Laurie the noise from the refrigerator bothers Beau and suggested she put a rug in front of it to help absorb the sound. He also hates the noise the ceiling fans make, but his parents have rectified that problem. They installed central air conditioning at no small expense!

Our conversation eventually turned to more common themes. "I love my green ones," Beau said, "but sometimes they take my green ones away."

Laurie looked puzzled for a moment and then laughed. "He means the avocados that fall off the tree," she said, smiling. "I take them away from him because they're fattening."

Beau also said he liked being in the big car with his Dad. Again, Laurie looked puzzled. "We have two SUVs," she said, "and they're the same size."

I asked Beau for clarification and he showed me the inside of a much bigger vehicle.

"It's the motor home!" Laurie said. "We don't keep it here and use it only occasionally, but the dogs have never been on a trip in it. They've just been inside it."

I advised her to take the boys for a ride in "the big car" and then on an overnight family outing. Animals love to be included.

Finally, we went into the back yard and out to the deck by the pool. Oscar and Felix were there, and they had a message for Laurie. They wanted her to know they were doing fine and were happy she was sharing her love with others of their kind.

"I've always known they were here," Laurie said with a smile.

That didn't surprise me at all.

Not Worthy

Ann and Pat adopted an 18-month-old black All-American dog from the Pound. Their German Shepherd, Gus, had taken Sam under his wing and showed her everything. It was obvious he loved her very much.

They were concerned because Sam acted as if she didn't want to be part of the family. She would look down and away when they glanced in her direction.

I always respect animals' personal space and wait for them to feel comfortable with me, and my first meeting with Sam was no exception. I sat on the floor a little ways from her and began our conversation.

She was looking down and away, and what she told me broke my heart.

"I am not worthy," she said. "My eyes are not worthy to look at."

I won't go into detail about the abuse she suffered before she came to this loving home, but suffice it to say she was made to feel that she didn't deserve to be alive.

"Your eyes are always worthy," I told her. "They are beautiful, and everyone here loves you and would be very pleased to look into your eyes. You are safe and you are loved."

I kept telling her these things and reassuring her, and eventually she came over and touched my cheek with her nose. Somehow I managed to hold back the tears, and I repeated that she had beautiful eyes.

Ann and Pat have the patience and love to help Sam overcome her feelings of inferiority, and I am so glad she is with them.

It's important for us all to remember that the reasons for an animal's actions are not always what they seem.

Daisy

I've been working with a Golden Retriever rescue group, helping these dedicated people who do their best to find good homes for dogs from the pound or dogs who've been left at their doorstep.

My role is to find out what happened to these animals before they were rescued, because that knowledge helps us understand their behavior and temperament issues.

Daisy was three years old when she came into the possession of the rescue group. Her owners had gotten another dog and had kicked Daisy out, claiming they were afraid she was going to bite their children.

The rescue group's procedure was to board a dog until it could be physically and mentally evaluated, then place the animal in an appropriate foster home until a "forever home" could be found.

Daisy's temperament problems were evident where she was boarded. She bit the groomer, but didn't break the skin, when he picked her up to put her in the bath. She told me she didn't like to be surprised by having someone approach her from the right. It appeared that she had no peripheral vision on that side.

The little Golden wanted to be an only dog, and several months later she was placed in a good home. Her new owner had his arm around her and was petting her feet when she nipped him. He brought her back to the rescue group.

Daisy didn't want to talk about the incident, so we took her to an eye specialist who said there was nothing wrong with her peripheral vision.

Desperate, we drove her to my longtime vet and friend, Dr. Fricks. We put a muzzle on her before taking her into the examining room.

Dr. Fricks is a very kind and gentle soul, and Daisy felt comfortable with him. He took the muzzle off; and then, finally, she showed me what had happened to her before she was rescued.

Her owners' two children had tied Daisy's back legs together, held them up in the air, and forced her to walk on her front legs as if she was a wheelbarrow. They had done this time and time again.

In her fear that it would happen to her yet again, Daisy was simply protecting herself.

It was a good reminder to us all that we need to give a new pet some space to adjust to its surroundings and human companions. There has to be a grace period to allow for the development of mutual trust and respect. Yes, we want to immediately smother them with affection, but it is best to let them come to us when they are ready.

Daisy has since been adopted by a kind, patient, dog-savvy family that knows her history. I believe she has found her forever home.

SILENT WORDS

Chapter 10
Healing with Captain

All dogs are descendents of wolves, and every wolf pack has at least one healer – a creature with special powers and the ability to heal his brethren if it is meant to be. Consequently, it should be no surprise that there are healers within the dog population.

Captain was turned over to Golden Retriever rescue at the age of 11 after he had been diagnosed with thyroid cancer. His family couldn't bear to watch him die. The rescue team's vet gave him two weeks to a month to live, so I took him home with me to make his final days as pleasant as possible.

My Airedale, McKenzie, accepted him immediately and they instantly became best friends. McKenzie knew that Captain needed to be with us, so he was generous with his time, food, toys, and anything else the old boy wanted.

Captain immediately stole my heart and was with me for nearly a year.

You see, it wasn't his time to go just yet, because he hadn't finished his task on this earth: teaching me to use my heretofore hidden ability to heal animals.

He was a sweet, gentle old soul – a Golden of great beauty even at his advanced age. Imagine my surprise when he revealed his intentions to me. McKenzie, of course, was not surprised.

After all, McKenzie is the second reincarnation of Winston, the Airedale who first helped me to acknowledge my gift and begin my life's work as an animal communicator. It's only appropriate that he be here for the second stage of my education, this time with Captain.

I must admit at first I was a bit nervous and doubtful that the ability to heal was somewhere within me, but Captain's gentle encouragement spurred me on.

If I told him about a particular animal with an ailment, he would either show me it was time for that soul to move on, or he would indicate that the creature was supposed to remain here in this physical world for a while. In non-life-threatening cases, he knew whether the animal might be cured or that healing was prohibited by "karma."

Captain taught me to pull that knowledge from myself, as well as how to use my hands on an area of distress to push away the heat emanating from it. And I learned to help animal owners think positively and thus provide an atmosphere more conducive to healing.

Once he was satisfied that I had learned my lessons well, Captain's beautiful soul moved on to the other side. He had developed a large tumor on his lung, and for two weeks I never left his side as he grew weaker and weaker. He wanted to go on his own terms. Finally, he lifted his head to once again lick the tears from my face, as the white light approached. And then he was gone, into the light.

My heart was broken, but I knew I had to go on. Captain had made it clear that he wanted me to take in rescued animals with medical problems and practice my new-found skills.

McKenzie and I miss his physical presence, but he will always – always — be in our hearts. And I will always remember the lessons he taught me as he guided me through the initial encounters with sick animals during the months we were together.

My first healing case arrived without warning and before I was even remotely sure of myself. I received an emergency call from the owner of Zandra, an older Lab with a serious and sudden case of pneumonia. Captain was at home and I was in the car, and he told me the dog was not supposed to move on and that I needed to put my hands on her. Zandra also told me she was not ready to go, so I drove to the animal hospital. I focused my energy and gently rubbed away the heat coming from her torso.

Her owner, Linda, told me later that the vets were amazed "Z" recovered so quickly. She was out of the hospital in a couple of days.

Nicky – a 15-years-young, black all-American dog with great scruffy whiskers and eyebrows – was my next patient. She had suddenly stopped walking, but she told me she wasn't ready to go. "I'm not done," she said. Captain confirmed that she belonged here a little longer and showed me where the acupuncturist should place the needles and where I should put my hands. Nicky is walking just fine now and continues with her acupuncture treatments.

A horse named Partner was having a bad time with painful hooves, and Captain showed me using a crystal to heal him. Yes, I have a crystal, given to me years ago by a mystic who said it "belonged" to me. Crystals are for healing and for information, but I had never considered using one to help heal anyone. Although I had not showed it to him, Captain knew I had it, and thankfully I was able to put Partner back on his feet.

And then it was Ellie's turn. She's my dapple-gray mini horse, and she had stopped eating. Captain showed me the problem was in her mouth and told me I needed to take care of it, so I trailered her to an equine hospital many miles away. Sure enough, she had an abscessed tooth, but the ailment turned out to be much more severe. The vet discovered that an earlier vet – long before Ellie became mine – had filled the little horse's sinuses with a liquid that hardened, presumably to plug a gap where another tooth had been lost. The material had to be chipped out and it took hours.

When the surgery was over, I put my hands on Ellie, and she told me she could smell me for the very first time. The unfairness of it all made me want to cry, but I tried to concentrate on the future and how much better she would feel.

I don't know what tomorrow will bring or how my new-found gift will improve the lives of the many animals I try to help. But I am prepared to do my best, and I will be forever grateful to Captain for showing me the way.

SILENT WORDS

Chapter 11
When Disaster Strikes

Many domesticated animals are displaced, lost, and separated from their families during natural disasters. After the event – whether it's a hurricane, fire, tsunami, earthquake or flood – Mother Nature's innocent creatures all feel the same way.

Fires in Southern California's ubiquitous mountains are not unusual, but that does not make them any less devastating for the animals living in the region.

Although we all would have wished for better circumstances, I had the opportunity to communicate with numerous animals during a recent wildfire in Los Angeles and Ventura counties.

When the fire began, I knew it was close to areas filled with ranches, stables, and private homes with barns. I also knew how difficult it is to move a number of horses at once. As the conflagration spread, I raced to a friend's stable to help.

Few ranches have enough trailers for all of their livestock at one time, so each horse had to be walked out of the area by one person. I could smell and see the smoke from the fire as we made our way out of the foothills to the valley below. The horse I had was confused and uneasy, so I told him "You need to do this right now and then everything will be fine." He settled down.

When we arrived at the evacuation center at a local community college, everything was in controlled chaos. Each horse was painted with a number for identification purposes and then turned out in a fenced open area. There was ample food and volunteers were already assembling, so I went back to the stable and walked out another horse. The fire was getting worse.

By the time I returned, there were about 100 horses plus goats, sheep, ponies, mules, donkeys, and even some pigs. And I knew there were equal numbers at another evacuation center across the valley.

Although the animals were being well cared for and were safe, they were extremely unhappy. I was hit by a barrage of jumbled pictures and I could feel their unease. This was where I was needed.

I joined the volunteers who were brushing, grooming, walking and feeding the horses, because those tasks needed to be done as well. As I worked with each animal, he or she told me the same thing: "I can't find my friends, my Mom and Dad aren't here, I'm in a strange place, and why am I not getting my special food?" Horses live to eat and are accustomed to grazing all day long. They were out of their normal environment and were totally stressed and overwhelmed.

I tried to get them into a calmer state of mind. "You need to be here at this time and then you'll go home," I explained to each one I could reach. "You're safe."

Usually, once a horse understands what it is you want him to do, he'll say, "OK, I can do that." But there was a lot of backsliding in this group situation. Another animal communicator arrived to help, but I don't think we were able to interact with every equine on the premises.

One bay gelding in particular sticks out in my mind. He stood off to the side, not engaging the other horses, and he was very sad. I asked him why. He said when he came to that place, he thought he was being reunited with his "other owner," but he couldn't find her. In truth, one of his two owners had died, but the horse never knew that and thought she was just "away." I explained that she was no longer in this physical world, and he accepted that; but the facts did not lighten his sadness. I wished I could do more for him, but I had to move on.

For three days, while the fire raged on, I drove back and forth between the two evacuation centers, attempting to calm the animals as best I could while I walked, brushed and fed them. I kept sending out the same message, and eventually it began to have the desired result.

Finally the wildfire was contained, and owners began to arrive to collect their livestock. The horses were very happy to be going home, and so was I.

It's amazing what animals think about in stressful situations. I can only imagine what was going through the minds of the thousands of creatures stranded in the wake of Hurricane Katrina. They weren't going home, because their homes were, for the most part, destroyed and their Moms and Dads missing. Thank goodness for all the volunteer groups, such as Best Friends, who rescued them and found them new homes.

SILENT WORDS

Chapter 12

Reunited at Last

The soul takes wing, soars
To the other side of eternity
Only to return
Jubilant
United with a kindred spirit.
'Til then, Sweet Dreams…
—Merry Shelburne

A Hard Road

I had taken my Airedale to the vet, whose office is located on a horse farm, and while I was there I decided to visit the residents of the barn.

A large brown horse was sending out a message that he had something to tell Nancy. She is co-owner of the clinic and performs veterinary acupuncture there, and she has been a lifelong horse person.

When I responded to Paint, he was quite excited about the prospect of communicating with a human. He told me he had been Nancy's horse in his previous life and their relationship had been interrupted by his untimely death. He had gone through many hardships to get back to her; but she did not recognize him, and this was a source of great frustration for him.

Nancy was amazed when I told her the story. Many horses had passed through her hands, but she didn't know which one had come back as Paint.

She told me he had been a very successful racehorse, albeit with a reputation for violence. Nancy had met Paint when he was purchased by a well-known racing farm, and she had even been called upon to save his life when Western (conventional) veterinary medicine had failed to cure a serious ailment.

When his racing career was over, the owners gave Paint to Nancy. She tried to train him in dressage, but his violence continued, and it seemed to be mixed with fear and anger.

"I often felt like he was trying to tell me something," she said, "but it was never clear."

Once I explained to Paint that Nancy now understood they had been together in his previous life, he continued to be frustrated because she didn't recognize him.

He kept saying to her, "I know who you are, so you must know me."

But that all changed a few months ago when Nancy had an epiphany.

One evening, in the quiet of his stall, Paint exhibited behavior he had never shown her before. He licked her neck and then nosed under her shirt and licked her stomach.

And then she suddenly recognized him. "You are Accoa!" she cried. Paint responded by moving his head around to hug her body tightly to his with his neck.

Nancy later told me she had never known such love and such peace as she did at that moment.

Accoa had been a successful racehorse in his own right, and he had been given to Nancy by the same farm that bought and raced him again as Paint. Accoa had died suddenly in mid-jump over a fence on a cross-country course. Nancy felt she had somehow killed him and had pushed his memory to the far corners of her mind.

Paint is no longer angry and violent, and he and Nancy are happily training in dressage. It was a long, hard journey, but he is home.

The Shadow

Slim was a herding dog, and he lived in a canyon house with his Mom. Most of the time he followed her around like a shadow, but almost every day he would take off into the canyons and return with a dead animal as a "gift" for her.

His owner wanted to understand his behavior.

"She doesn't get it," Slim told me. "When she does, then I won't have to be her shadow."

I asked him to explain and he said, "When she took me out of the trash can, I told her you finally found me. You've been looking for me for years."

When I passed along this information, the woman confirmed that she had found Slim in a trash can, where he had been discarded as a puppy. But she didn't understand the significance.

"I told her from the very beginning," Slim continued. "The last time you saw me, I was in the trash can in the back of the pickup truck, and you were standing on the street, crying."

When I told her this, the woman was absolutely still for five minutes, and then the tears began.

"When I was about 12," she explained, "I had a cat that clung to me all the time. I loved that cat. When he died, my Dad tossed him into the trash in the back of the truck and drove away."

Slim has no need to shadow his Mom any more, because now she "gets it." But she has built a fence along the property line to keep him close to her and to keep him safe. She doesn't want to lose that little soul again.

Chance

Cindy, a semi-retired stunt woman, had been a client of mine for years. She bought a five-year-old horse named Cosmo and then called me to come over to the stable and make sure he was happy with his new arrangements.

She had renamed him Chance. "When I met him, I knew I had to have him," she explained. "I don't know why."

She was hoping he'd enjoy riding in shows with her.

"Tell my new Mom I knew her when she could only brush my stomach," Chance announced.

The message surprised her and made her stop and think.

Chance showed me the red-handled curry brush she had used in his former life, and I described it to Cindy. He also showed me

Cindy and her sister as little girls, the view from his barn stall, and the team roping job he'd had chasing cattle.

"That's when we won the red blanket," he insisted.

Her father had been a rodeo rider and stunt man, and Cindy was remembering a horse from her childhood.

"His name was Dandy," she said, "and I really loved him. I spent a lot of time with him."

Cindy's father had died when she was 19, and her Mom had sold Dandy.

"I really wasn't yours," Chance interjected, "but I was a part of you."

Now she was positive this was the horse. She began to cry, sobbing, and she couldn't stop.

I asked her why tears were falling at such a potentially happy moment.

"I want to call my Mom and sister," she explained between sobs, "and there's no cell phone reception here. I want to call them right now, because they'll remember where Dandy went."   They were tears of momentary frustration… and joy.

When she did reach her family, they told her that the man who purchased Dandy had kept him until the horse passed away eight years ago. Her Mom and sister also confirmed the existence of the red Navajo blanket that Cindy's father used on Dandy. The blanket hadn't been "won" but was a gift from Native Americans living on a reservation in New Mexico, where Dad was working as a stunt man on a movie. It was a sign of respect for his horsemanship.

Cindy looked through her old family photos and found a picture of her father and Dandy in a roping competition. A copy of that photo now hangs in Chance's tack trunk, reminding them both of the time when a little girl sat in his stall and told him bedtime stories about "Cinderella Filly."

You'll Find Me by Accident

My long-time client Julie had a Golden Retriever mix from a previous marriage. Even though Maxie was closer to her ex-husband, the dog stayed with her.

When it was time for the 15-years-young canine to cross over, Julie wanted to know if and when she would come back to her. I said we would know two weeks after she passed.

Maxie left in April, and two weeks later she told me that her soul would be back during the "cool time."

"Tell her she'll find me just by accident and I'll be in a box," she said.

The dog was coming back to Julie because it was their time to be together.

From August to November, Julie called me almost weekly on my cell phone. "When will I find my new dog?" she kept asking. She was going to Pounds and rescue organizations and actively looking for the pup.

I reminded her that she would find her new dog "by accident" and that it would be during cool weather.

One day she and her daughter, Dana, took a wrong turn on the freeway and somehow ended up in Pasadena, where they drove past the Pasadena Humane Society.

"Let's look in there!" her daughter suggested.

I received a phone call shortly thereafter.

When I arrived at the Humane Society, Julie and Dana were looking at two "All-American" puppies in a cage. Dana was positive that one of them was their new dog.

"It's the black one on the left," I confirmed. That little soul had come back to them.

As Julie was signing the papers, the desk clerk mentioned that the puppies had arrived in a box.

The new Mom named her new-old dog Maggie, and they are inseparable. She takes her everywhere and they love each other very much.

Amazing Revelation

Trudy and her husband had a beautiful gray cat named Eva, and they lived in a two-story home. As is sometimes the case, the couple decided to separate. During the divorce proceedings, he took Eva with him in his motor home.

Each time he stopped, he would let the feline out to run around. Trudy had been in touch with him by phone, and she kept telling him it was dangerous to let Eva out unsupervised. She worried, and one day her fears were realized. The gray cat did not return to the motor home.

Moving on, Trudy put her grief behind her, found a new place to live, and adopted a pure black kitty she named Negri. When I visited, Negri revealed that she was Eva. She had come back because "we didn't get a chance to finish what we started."

Trudy nodded and smiled when I told her this, but I felt she really didn't understand what had happened. Not in her heart.

A couple of years later, Trudy adopted another cat she named Sofie. The three of them lived peacefully together, and I visited every once in awhile.

Two more years passed, and one day I received a call from Trudy that was different from the others. She had concern in her voice. Sofie, she said, would turn a corner in the house, come upon Negri, and start freaking out. Sofie would jump, run away, and want nothing to do with Negri; and Trudy wanted to know what was going on.

"I see the gray," Sofie told me.

Negri was showing herself as gray instead of black, and that was confusing and scary to Sofie.

But it was an exciting revelation to me! Up until then, I didn't know animals could do that. Apparently Negri can hold the gray form for just a short period of time, because only Sofie has seen her that way.

Negri told me she was showing herself as gray so Trudy would understand that she really was Eva's little soul.

"Tell my Mom," she said, "that she became a stronger person, a better person. I'm happy for her because she turned things around."

Trudy got it then. Negri truly was Eva. And even though they had been reunited for four years, this was the first time Trudy really understood.

Seeing that recognition in Trudy's eyes was a gift for me. These are the things that make what I do so fulfilling.

When the Rains Came

Krissy and Scott had two elderly dogs who crossed over to the other side within a month of each other. Rudy the German Shepherd left in June and Yana followed in July.

In August, Krissy was having a difficult time coping with the loss of her two beloved dogs, so she gave me a call and I went out to the house.

Although Yana did not make an appearance, Rudy was there. And he had good news!

He told me he would be born by the end of the year, that Krissy and her husband would find him "when it was pouring rain all the time," and that there was some connection to "up North."

Since it was So. California, both Krissy and I doubted it would be "pouring rain all the time," so we thought perhaps he would be in Oregon or Washington.

In the beginning of 2005, it started to rain in So. California, and it rained for almost three months. Houses were sliding down hillsides, sink holes were opening in streets, freeways were buried in water.

January brought news from Scott's sister, who lives in the So. California desert. A litter of German Shepherds had been born nearby on Dec. 30. Both the sire and dam were from northern states.

Krissy contacted the breeder, who emailed her photos of the litter.

"I knew which one he was," Krissy said. "I printed his picture and hung it on my office wall."

They picked up Rudy Boy in late February and brought him home.

I had told them in August that Rudy said when he came back he wanted to sleep in the bed and eat Scott's tortilla chips. Despite the current consensus about crating puppies, Rudy #2 refuses. Guess where he sleeps?

"When I look into his eyes, I see my Rudy there," Krissy wrote in a letter. "I'm in a state of disbelief and yet in my heart I believe it's him."

I went to visit when he was about seven months old, and Rudy Boy greeted me cheerfully.

"When I saw you last time I couldn't jump up," he announced, proudly showing off his newfound agility. In his previous life he had developed hip dysplasia.

He had more to say: "I know I promised that the yard was going to be my Dad's this time, but I need one place for myself."

So now the backyard has a hole for Rudy Boy to dig — a hole surrounded by beautiful plants.

But he has kept his promises: The shrubs and flowers are untouched, and there are tortilla chip crumbs in the bed.

No Time to Cover... continued

As you'll recall, Megan missed her old friend Patrick after he crossed to the other side. He had taught her many valuable things, and now she was anxious to mentor a new kitty.

Before he left this physical world, Patrick told me he would return and that he'd meet his Mom at Best friends, an animal rescue facility in Utah. As it happens, Mary goes there every year for a week to volunteer, so this time she was especially looking forward to the trip.

Sure enough, she'd been there no time at all when a very persistent kitty attached herself to Mary. Patrick had come back as... Patty!

"Thank you for my new ups," Patty announced. Somehow she knew that Mary had just bought another cat tree.

I'm guessing that Megan told Patty before Mary made her journey to Best Friends. And the two cats are, indeed, best friends in their new life together.

Chapter 13
Wisdom from the Heart

One of the most remarkable things I've learned about animals is that they have a sweet, startling, and always unexpected perspective on life. Their wisdom is so true, so unencumbered by human emotion, that I am often taken aback by their messages.

The Cage

It was a lovely spring afternoon, and I had the front door open to let in the fresh, cool air. My little lovebird's cage was in the living room, and she was enjoying the day as much as I was.

Then I noticed my Airedale Maxwell sitting on the floor and looking up at her.

Needing to know what was going on between the two of them, and hoping not to see a picture of the bird in the dog's mouth(!), I sat down and got involved in their conversation.

What a wise old soul that little bird was!

Maxwell was bragging about all the places he went in the car, all the things he got to do in his yard and the house, and all the other fun things in his life.

He told her she had only her cage and that was where she needed to be.

After Maxwell finished bragging to her, the bird looked down at him and said, "We all live in a cage. Only some are bigger than others."

I will never forget that special afternoon and the lesson I learned from that little bird.

We all live in our own kind of cage, and we should never brag about things we have, because what another has might be just as important. It all depends on your perspective.

Kisses

Big Jim was a beautiful Rottie, and his human companions wanted to know if he liked the family's new car.

Rottweilers are naturally gentle, affectionate animals who respond to love with adoration. The breed has an undeserved reputation in some quarters because a few have been trained to be guard dogs. But I digress...

I went to visit them on a cold, rainy day, but the weather didn't matter to Jim. He told me he loved the new car because he could see out the windows.

We sat in the living room and chatted for a while, and Jim walked over to his Dad and licked the side of his face. Dad reacted by hugging him and planting kisses all over the top of Jim's head, much to the dog's delight.

Jim's Dad then wiped his wet cheek on his sleeve. It was a natural enough gesture for a human, but the Rottie immediately wanted to know why.

"I don't wipe off his kisses," Jim said, "so why did he wipe off mine?"

It was a good question, and I didn't have a good answer; but it really made me stop and think about the little things that mean so much to our animal companions. They instinctively know what is important in life.

I finally told him his Dad didn't wipe off the kiss; he just had an itch he needed to scratch.

Weeds

Candice was a lovely, pampered white cat with blue eyes who lived in a beautiful garden. It sounds like the beginning of a fairy tale, doesn't it?

But this particular kitty would bring weeds into the house and leave them in the middle of the kitchen floor. Never plants or flowers – just weeds.

Her Mom was a serious gardener and her flower beds and shrubs were immaculate, so it drove her crazy trying to figure out why Candice kept doing this. Was the feline trying to tell her that she should weed more often? And how did the cat know which were flowers and which were weeds?

Eventually, I was summoned to solve the puzzle.

The answer was both simple and complex.

"My Mom didn't plant these," Candice explained, "so I bring them in to her. Only the Spirit can grow a weed. It is a gift. There is no 'weed seed.'"

Years later, a wolf named Durango told me the same thing. He said that the "hairless ones" (humans) are afraid of what grows from the earth unless they planted it, while wolves love everything that the earth produces because it gives them good health.

I've been reluctant to pull up a weed ever since.

Extreme Pampering

I got a call from Joan about her two-and-a-half-year-old tabby cat, Roger. She was worried because he slept all the time and wasn't interested in chasing birds or doing any of the other things cats usually do.

When she opened the door at my knock, the smallest cat I'd ever seen was cradled in the crook of her arm.

"This is my boy Roger," she said, introducing us. He blinked at me sleepily.

I glanced around the house for possible clues to environmental causes of his malaise. The evidence was ample.

Cat beds and cat trees were everywhere. There were water bowls in every corner. One whole cupboard was filled with cat food. It was totally a cat house for just one kitty.

As Joan and I chatted, she revealed that she always took his food to him and she was constantly carrying and cuddling him.

Her motivation was love: she wanted to protect him because he was so small.

Roger was experiencing no discomfort and no depression. I asked him how he felt about always being held.

"I know nothing else," he said. "Outside is dangerous."

I advised Joan to stop carrying Roger around, to let him go to his food and water bowls rather than bring them to him, and to allow him to explore his back yard.

"You haven't let him be a cat," I explained to her. "He's never experienced what life is all about. What if something happened to you? He wouldn't be capable of coping."

During the ensuing months, Joan made steady progress toward undoing the effects of extreme pampering.

When I visited a year later, Roger's entire personality had changed to one of exuberance.

"He makes me laugh with his antics!" Joan exclaimed. "He's interested in everything."

Roger could hardly wait to show me all of the neat things in his yard, his little hidey-holes where he could watch the birds, and his outdoor toys.

I was so happy to see that the change had enhanced the quality of both their lives.

Brock O. Lee

Dr. Fricks, who is a veterinarian, and his wife Gracie are dear friends of mine, and they call me in whenever they think I can help with a situation.

This time it was one of their own animals who was in trouble, and I was more than happy to serve as a communication conduit between them and their Doberman, Brock. O. Lee.

Brock was just 7 years old and weighed 70 pounds when a 5-year-old, 100 pound Dobie broadsided him in the multi-dog household. Gunther didn't mean to injure Brock. He was just in a hurry to greet Mom and Dad when they came home from work, and Brock was in the way.

After the collision, Brock struggled to get up, but he could not. A myliogram the following day revealed a severe compression on his spinal cord, and immediate surgery was needed to relieve the pressure.

Dr. Fricks and Gracie called me in to talk to Brock O. Lee. He said he was willing to try if they were. His eyes were bright and alert, even though he was uncomfortable and knew it was going to be a long road to recovery.

During the weeks that followed the surgery, they transported Brock and his IV equipment back and forth every day between the hospital and home. This included carrying him up and down a flight of stairs. Gracie slept on the couch every night to be near him. He was stable but he could not walk or even stand for more than a few minutes.

Complications ensued that included swollen extremities and a feeding tube in his stomach, among other problems. Gracie feared that the end might be near.

I went to see him again, and Brock told me he was still willing to go on. "I'm not going anywhere," he said firmly.

That gave Mom and Dad hope. After some medical procedures were tried, Brock finally started to eat on his own, and with each day he grew stronger. Gradually he was able to struggle to his feet, even though it was painful, and eventually he began to take a few tentative steps. There was no stopping him then.

Brock kept reassuring me that he was in it for the long haul. He was loved and he knew it, and his job for this lifetime was not finished.

The staff at Dr. Fricks' clinic showed their love for the Dobie by worked tirelessly with him during the days, helping and encouraging him to move forward.

And then, several months after the initial accident, he was walking again.

He taught everyone involved a valuable lesson: never, ever give up.

Brock O. Lee enjoyed another year of happiness and love with his family before his condition returned and he told me he was ready to go. It was time.

There wasn't a dry eye in the place, except his. And no one will forget everything that beautiful soul taught us.

SILENT WORDS

Chapter 14
Crossing Over

I learned early on that animals accept death as a natural part of life, and when they are ready to cross over to the other side, they are... ready! They look upon our futile efforts to prolong their lives as understandable but wasted effort. They are at peace.

Unselfish Deeds

It was an early Saturday morning in April when their Doberman, Gunther, woke up Gracie to let him go out. His feet sensed the dew on the grass that covered his pads. He stood looking into the darkness of the night, making sure his yard was still safe for all. He then walked back across the yard, stopping once again to take a deep breath of that crisp morning air. Knowing it would be his last morning in this physical world, he truly wanted to enjoy it, for he loved that part of the day so much.

As he entered the back door, he thanked Gracie for loving him and for being so patient while he enjoyed his yard for the last time. He made his way to his bed and curled up in it, knowing his beloved friends were with him, and took his last breath. At seven years young, he moved on to the other side.

I want to thank Gunther for sharing his last minutes and teaching me that "Eyes do not need tears in them to be sad."

One's world can change as quickly as an ocean wave crashing onto the sand. The sound is as loud as the soul is strong. Once the sound is gone, the soul moves on. Dr Frics and Gracie found themselves standing at that shoreline that morning, and as the sound turned to silence, so did their world.

When one stands in that moment in time, the world is silenced. There are no words to be heard, no minutes that turn into hours. The wave of that soul now rushes through our memories. It is truly one of the quietest times in life, a time where we stand alone within ourselves, knowing there is nothing on the outside that can change the void in our heart. We are truly alone.

Now, feeling the loss of one of their beloved friends, who left them so fast at such a young age, Dr. Fricks and Gracie put their hearts and Gunther's beloved soul on hold. They drove to the veterinary hospital that morning to do what they do best, be there for us. With heart in hand and tears that would not fall that day for them, they unselfishly walked our loving pets into a healthy and more comfortable place. I personally cannot think of two other people who are so compassionate that they would put their lives on hold in order to have ours move forward in such a positive way.

We have vets who treat and get attached to all of our pets on a daily basis. They feel our losses much more than we know. Yet they continue to be there for us, knowing animals have only one fault: they never live long enough. The minute they enter our lives, we are headed for heartache.

We are blessed to have these special souls in our lives.

So the next time you are at your vet's office, remember this story and thank him or her for being there for you and your beloved pet.

I Don't Want Another Dog

My sister, Claudia, and her husband, Steve, had a buff-colored Cocker Spaniel named Buffy who loved and spent equal time with both of them. She was a very special girl who was loved dearly in return.

On a warm August morning, when she was 13 years young, Buffy developed a heart problem that affected her breathing. They rushed her to an emergency clinic, and the vets recommended she be taken to a heart specialist many miles away.

Steve and Claudia didn't hesitate for a second. They drove Buffy immediately to the specialist, but nothing could be done. They had to set Buffy free.

After a period of grieving for their girl, Claudia began to look for another dog. She needed someone to fill the void.

But Steve was adamant: "I don't want another dog. It's too soon."

Nevertheless, Claudia dragged him to numerous pet adoption events. She usually dragged me along, too. Steve continued to be resistant to the whole idea and would ignore the dogs Claudia suggested.

Eventually we went to an adoption clinic in a large park. About an hour into the event, I spotted a mostly black Terrier mix up on a hill and suggested that Claudia go take a look. As usual, Steve refused to accompany her.

Claudia made an instant connection with the year-old female and insisted that Steve meet her. When he did, when he touched her, his whole attitude changed.

There was a two-day delay before they could bring her home, and Steve was so excited he could hardly wait. He went shopping and bought her a bed, collar, and all kinds of toys.

They named her Molly, and when they took her home, I was there to provide a communication conduit while she adjusted to her new environment.

As I was about to leave, Molly said to me, "Can you tell them that Buffy sent me to be with them, because they need one of my kind to take care of them while she is gone."

With a lump in my throat, I passed along the message.

Steve had a special crate and bed built to go in their camper. Molly goes everywhere with them, and she's doing an excellent job of providing comfort and joy to her adoptive parents.

Love just goes on, from one soul to another.

Murphy

When the phone rang at 7 p.m., I knew what it meant. And my heart broke for them, because I knew their time together was coming to an end.

Animals always seem to know what is best for us, and that was the case with Murphy, a black all-American dog who became Lisa's companion when she really needed a special soul in her life.

As their years together unfolded, their love and respect for one another was obvious for all to see. Their bond was almost palpable, and Murphy had taken on the job of protecting Lisa from all real or perceived dangers.

I would be meeting with clients at Lisa's barn, and I'd see them together. Murphy was always at her side, and I could feel the trust and love between them.

One evening Lisa was on her way into a sports event. As she was walking away from her car, leaving Murphy inside as always, she heard a voice say, "You should not leave your dog in the car."

Before Lisa had a chance to tell the man that Murphy would be OK, he walked over to the car and put his hand through the open window to see if the dog was cool and safe. Knowing how overprotective Murphy was, Lisa was sure the stranger would be bitten. Instead, the dog was licking his hand.

Lisa was shocked because this had never happened before. Murphy always showed her teeth and was ready to attack any stranger who came close to her Mom or the car.

It turned out the man was a police officer, and Murphy sensed that protective side of him. She approved because she knew he could help her take care of Lisa.

Not long after that, Lisa and Vinny were married, and with Murphy at their side they started a new life together. They bought a ranch so they could board horses who needed to recover from surgery or were taking a break from training.

Vinny worked hard on the ranch, with Murphy helping as much as she could. But you could still catch the dog lying in the shade, watching Lisa give jumping lessons and making sure she was safe. You see, she loved her Dad, but Murphy's eyes would sparkle when she was with Mom.

Time passed, and when Murphy was 12 she developed cancer. Then it was Lisa's and Vinny's turn to protect her, and they did everything possible to keep that beloved soul moving forward in comfort.

Murphy told me she was more than willing to go along with the plan. Even though she found it harder to get up and move around, she still went to work with Lisa and worked the ranch with Vinny. She was enjoying every minute she had left in this physical world, because her love for them reached beyond her discomfort.

As I drove to the veterinary hospital that night after the phone call, I thought of the emotions that Lisa and Vinny were facing. They were about to enter a place that numbs the mind and leaves the soul feeling helpless: the darkest of tunnels, where time has no mercy and no warmth.

With her eyes half open, Murphy told me she was ready. She had done her job. She had found Vinny, and she knew he would take care of Lisa while she was gone. Then she said, "Could you thank my Mom for letting me walk through this life with her by my side."

I can still see Murphy trotting around the ranch grounds or just lying in the shade watching Lisa give lessons at the barn. And I know in my heart that someday that little soul will return in a new form, eager to spend another lifetime with her beloved friends.

Menagerie of Friends

A woman with 12 cats and 2 dogs asked me to come and talk to all her animals, and one in particular caught my attention. He was an ancient and very frail feline curled up in a stuffed chair that had a heating pad to warm his bones.

But he was a trooper. He left his cozy perch and made his way down the hall to the room where we had all gathered, because he wanted to make sure each creature had his or her say.

All of them said they were sorry that Mom had lost her husband the previous year, and it was obvious that they all got along and loved each other.

As I asked the woman the names of her pets, I pointed to one and said, "Who is that orange cat?"

She said there was no orange cat, and I assured her there was. She thought for a moment and then realized it was the kitty who had crossed over 5 years earlier.

I also told her there was a soul with a lot of feathers, perhaps a rooster. That one stumped her for a while, and then she remembered the rooster who had been part of the family long ago.

A week later she called me and said the old cat was curled up on her bed. One by one, each of his family members had sat on the bed next to him and then departed. Although she suspected the worst, she wanted to know what it meant.

I had to do this on the phone, as time was short, and the old guy told me he was ready to go. He had just one request: he wanted to cross over at home rather than at a vet's office. His friends had said their goodbyes, and the orange cat and the rooster were there to assist his move to the other side. He was at peace.

From previous experience with many other animals, I knew the cat and rooster were there to help him go through the white light. They have shown it to me. The light has a power and brightness that is overwhelming, but at the same time it is calm and peaceful.

I assured the woman that the experience would be painless for this little soul. In fact, it would be pleasant, and perhaps some day he would return to help another through the light.

She let him go. Not without tears, but she let him go.

Chapter 15
Fuzzibear's Tale

They're all special in their own way, but sometimes I have the privilege of knowing a truly memorable dog. Prince Fuzzibear O'Hara, a.k.a. The FuzzMonster, was one-of-a-kind...not because of anything special he accomplished, but simply because of the sheer force of his personality.

I first met Fuzzibear and his Mom, Merry, when he was about 8 years old. He had a Golden Retriever pedigree, but he wasn't a show or performance dog. He was just a dog...with great intelligence, an iron will, and a wicked sense of humor.

Fuzzibear was an accomplished thief. Anything not beyond his reach was in peril. For example, one night his Dad, Dave, brought home 3 casaba melons in a plastic bag. They were very heavy, so he set them on the floor, reasoning that Fuzzy could not possibly carry them away. In the next instant, Fuzzy was carrying the bag out through the doggy door. Merry made a grab for him, but she was laughing too hard to hold on. They picked up flashlights and ran out to the back yard, where they found him smacking his lips over a mostly devoured melon. He wasn't in the least bit abashed.

On another occasion, they were missing an entire bunch of bananas. Outside the back door, placed precisely in the middle of the mat, Merry found the still-intact 5 stems. And lest you think that fruit was the only thing he stole and destroyed, they kept a list on a blackboard for all to see. It included a 5-pound Thesaurus, an $800 pair of contact lenses, a bag of small Christmas baskets filled with goodies, numerous remote controls, glasses (the kind you drink out of), glasses (the kind you wear on your face), scissors, hand saw, flashlight, silverware, work gloves, wrapped gifts... You name it, he stole it and ate it.

Fuzzibear was a master of misdirection. He would cause a disturbance in one place that would bring them running, to lament over some disaster; and while they were preoccupied with that, he would sneak into some forbidden territory and eat a shoe.

If their agility girl, Goldie, had a toy he wanted, he would introduce a different toy and literally wave it in front of her until she dropped the one she had. And then he'd smugly give her the new one and grab the one he wanted.

Fuzzibear re-decorated their house. By the time he was finished with a rectangular coffee table, it was oval. He ate part of a brick wall. He brought entire tree limbs in through the doggy door and topped them off with pillows from their bed.

He was a braggart. Merry took Fuzz for a walk every day, and I accompanied them on several occasions. He would brag to each dog he passed, giving them a condescending stare, raising his tail and strutting. Of course, the dogs behind gates and fences did not take kindly to this behavior and voiced their disapproval. Another older Golden lived just up the street, and he and Fuzzy had an ongoing conversation through the gate.

"I'm on a walk and you're not."

"You can't come in here. This is mine."

"Oh, yes, I can."

"No, you can't."

"Yes, I can. My Mom can bring me right in there if I want."

Fuzz had a way of looking at you that was a bit unnerving. He would sit and stare at you out of the corner of his eyes, his pink tongue hanging out, with a look on his face that was bored, wise and amused all at once. I knew he was always thinking about what mischief he could get into, so when I was left alone with him for a few minutes, I would panic. Most of Dave and Merry's house was "dog proofed," put there would be several things left carelessly within his reach because I was there.

When Merry left the room, Fuzzy would say, "I'm going to see what I can find in her bag!"

And I would say, patting the couch next to me, "Why don't you come over here and see me instead? I have a good toy."

And he'd say, "No! I want to pull stuff out of her bag and find something to steal while she's not looking. Because I can."

Before I could get to him, he'd grab whatever interested him and trot nonchalantly out of the room with it.

"Fuzzy," I would say, running after him in desperation, "do you want to trade? Do you want a 'nanner?" He would never let go of anything in his mouth unless you offered a trade, but you'd still have to catch him first!

Fuzzibear also was a hunter. Squirrels chattered at him from the pine trees, knowing they dare not touch the ground. Raccoons taunted him from outside – and sometimes atop – the fence. Alas, the possums were not so swift or fortunate. He would bring Merry a prize, in the middle of the night, and she would screech at Dave to please dispose of the gift. Dave always told her it was "playing possum" and wasn't really dead. Yes, the back yard was Fuzzy's kingdom, and he ruled it with an iron paw.

Fuzzy the Dog was somewhat famous. His face graced the cover of the first edition of this book in 2004. And he was one of the official "pickers" in a weekly pro football prediction contest among area sportswriters. His photo was right there along with all the others in the L.A. Daily News. The funny thing was that he actually did choose which teams were going to win each weekend. Dave would hold a small cube of cheese in each hand and offer them both to Fuzzy. If Fuzz chose the cheese in the left hand, that meant he was predicting the home team would win. If he chose the cheese in the right hand, it was the visiting team. Fuzzy took this very seriously and debated over each choice. Oddly, he was among the most accurate pickers for most of the season.

Fuzzibear was expensive. He was dysplastic, which required special supplements and frequent chiropractic treatments and acupuncture. He was epileptic, which required regular medication. And when he was 7, he ate a wire barbecue brush, unbeknownst to his parents, and that resulted in a 2-week hospital stay, 3 surgeries, and a $13,000 bill. When he was nearly 12, he was diagnosed with squamous cell carcinoma in his nose. The 22 days of radiation, at a cost of $7,000, only stopped the cancer for 6 weeks. It ate away his nose, and yet his iron will never waned. He continued to insist on his daily walks, albeit much slower, and he never lost his enthusiasm for food.

Right before he started the radiation, I asked him to choose from among several healing crystals. He had a strong reaction to one, and I instructed Merry and Dave to hold it each time he underwent treatment. After the radiation was complete, they were to attach it to his collar. Every few days they had to bury it in the earth or lay it in the rain on something natural for a few hours so it could regain its energy. They did this faithfully, even though at first they weren't 100 percent convinced it would help. They (usually Dave) also spent 2-3 hours a day for nearly 5 weeks, in heavy rush-hour traffic, driving Fuzzy back and forth to the radiation clinic. Such is the devotion of the human-animal bond.

The last 8 months of his life Fuzz endured The Puppy, a sweet but high-spirited boy who stole Fuzzibear's food right out of his mouth and slept on top of him. Fuzzy allowed all this without complaint. Towards the end, when Dandy and Goldie would come home from an agility trial, Dandy would run immediately to find Fuzz and make sure he was OK. They had a special relationship, this grumpy old mentor and affectionate student. Fuzzers instructed him in the art of taking care of Merry, thievery, and shredding toilet paper.

Fuzzibear's iron will and determination to live was amazing. As the cancer ate away more and more of his nose, he simply adjusted. His daily walks became slower and slower because he could only breathe by panting, but he insisted on going anyway. His teeth became exposed on one side and he could no longer chew his raw bones. His parents substituted carrots. His nose got infected and they added an antibiotic to his supplements, and when that one stopped working they tried a stronger one. The smell permeated the house, but they got used to it. His eyes became infected and they used an ointment to keep them clear. He lost weight and muscle mass. Still he persevered, because to him this was just another bump on the road of life.

Finally, he stopped eating and seemed too weak to go on a walk. Merry was sure this was the end and told him it was OK. But when she called me, I said he was telling me that he wanted yogurt, sweet potatoes and cooked meat. She tried it and he gobbled it right down. With the holistic vet's blessing, she stopped the antibiotics and all the supplements except for the most crucial. She hand fed him every meal slathered in yogurt, and he ate with great gusto. They went on little walks, and he made it up and down the stairs by himself, although it was a struggle. The vet pronounced his lungs clear and his heart strong. He made it to the one-year anniversary of his diagnosis, and still he was determined to stay.

"He's teaching me patience, an attribute I've lacked my entire life," Merry wrote to her friends in the Canine Cancer internet group. "And he's providing an awesome example of perseverance and inner strength. I raise a toast to Fuzzibear... my hero."

Fuzzy went downhill very fast after that. Within two days of the anniversary, he was no longer ambulatory. His parents tried putting a towel under him to lift his back legs, but they were not weight-bearing. To make matters worse, the cancer had affected his eyes and he could barely see. Merry had to put the water bowl under his chin so he could drink.

"It's day-to-day now," I told her Friday night. It was a pleasant evening, so Dave carried him to the back deck and settled him on a comfy mat. When Merry went to check on him a while later, she discovered that Dandy had left his two favorite toys next to Fuzzy. It was the little guy's tribute to his mentor. "Just in case you need them," Dandy had told him.

The next time Merry went to check, Fuzzibear wasn't there. Dandy was looking down the deck stairs, so she turned on the light, and Fuzz was about 3/4 of the way down, just lying there and looking around. His front paw was caught in a crack between the steps. Dave worked his paw loose and carried him the rest of the way because it was obvious that he wanted to stay outside. They brought him fresh water and left him.

Saturday morning he was 50 feet away in the back yard. I don't know exactly how he did it, just that it involved great physical effort. That's all he showed me, and he told me he wanted to lie in the cool dirt and pine needles, and he made it happen. He was very tired, and overwhelmed with the realization that this bump in the road was really a barrier. He was ready and wanted to go, and I told Merry it was time. She made arrangements to take him to the vet's office Sunday afternoon. Originally she had planned to have the vet come to her home, but the pet crematorium wasn't open on the weekend and she had no place to keep him. The vet had facilities to handle it.

Somehow Fuzzibear knew this and he told me he planned it that way. You see, he loved going to the vet's office, which is on a horse farm. He loved the smells of the horses and chickens, and he loved lying on the acupuncturist's couch with his head in Merry's lap as she stroked his head and ears. She called it his "Spa Day" and he looked forward to it every two weeks. That's where he wanted to say goodbye. He had manipulated things, as usual, to get his way. And, oddly, that's where I had met him some four years earlier.

Fuzzy spent Sunday morning resting peacefully on a cushion in front of the bedroom fireplace. The house, or at least the rooms in which he had spent most of his time, was inexplicably filled with flies. There were no open doors or windows, and Merry was perplexed and outraged. She grabbed a flyswatter and went to work on the intruders. After an hour or so, she became convinced that the flies were a manifestation of the toxins and "bad things" leaving his body. She was right.

Fuzzibear's spirit floated free at 3 p.m. Sunday afternoon, his head in Merry's lap, his crystal lying on his neck. The spirits of a red Golden, a dark cat and a lighter cat had arrived a few minutes earlier to take him home. As I described them to Merry, she said they were Woof, Lampwick and Churchill, all previous members of the family.

Fuzzers asked me to thank his Mom and Dad for always allowing him to "let the monster out" when he couldn't control his "bad" behavior. And he wanted to thank Merry for the "special" she hand-fed him the last few weeks of his life. He liked that.

Just before he went to sleep, a human spirit arrived who Fuzzy described as "ornery." She said she wasn't that way anymore, and it was her turn to take care of him. Merry looked startled when I told her. She said it had to be her Mom, who had passed away more than 4 years ago and had been very fond of Fuzzibear. And yes, she was ornery.

I told Merry and Dave that Fuzzy's spirit would pass through his crystal when he crossed over, and that the crystal would be hot to the touch. It was. Merry clipped some of his beautiful golden fur to keep and kissed him on the top of his head. It was all very peaceful, but there wasn't a dry eye in the room, including mine. We all knew that Fuzzibear was one of a kind.

His mat remained in front of their bedroom fireplace, and the next morning they found that Dandy had brought in a small tree branch and left it precisely in the middle of the mat. In the months they'd been together, Fuzz had spent a lot of time showing Dandy all the things he needed to learn to make Merry smile. It worked.

That afternoon, 24 hours after he had crossed over, Fuzzibear continued with his main job, which was watching over Merry's emotional well being. He wanted her to know he had made the trip successfully, and he wanted her to feel the peace that he felt. He sent her a very strong image of himself at a younger age, along with the touch of his fur, and wrapped her in the warmth of his contentment. The visit lasted about a half hour while she worked at her computer.

"I just sat there and smiled and smiled," she told me later. "At first I thought I was imagining it. I couldn't actually *see* him, but I could see him sharply in my head. He was giving me that Fuzzy look. And I felt as if I could just move my arm a little and brush against his fur. And there was this tangible sensation of peace wrapped around me. I knew it was weird, but it didn't *feel* weird. It felt right."

And it was. A few months before Fuzzibear left us, he and Merry were on a walk at dusk and they turned a corner to see a huge full moon hanging in the sky. Inspired by the sight, Merry immediately told him that he was going to be her "Man in the Moon" and that every time the moon was full, they would reconnect.

They do. Of course, now she realizes that it was Fuzzy who put the idea in her head.

Chapter 16
The Wolves Sing

It was one of those gorgeous Southern California Spring mornings, complete with blue skies and wispy white clouds, when the four of us set out for Wolf Mountain Sanctuary.

My co-conspirator, Merry Shelburne, and her husband, Dave, joined Nancy Evans and myself for the two-hour drive. Nancy was one of the pioneers in veterinary acupuncture and also happened to be the only one of us who had previously encountered a wolf.

We had no idea what to expect. I had learned about Wolf Mountain when I bought some paintings of wolves at a pet expo. The artist, Trudy Estes, told me about the sanctuary, and I felt those creatures calling me. I had to go.

Wolf Mountain Sanctuary is located in the California high desert on a piece of land that bears no resemblance to a mountain. The last 100 yards of bumpy road is dirt and rocks. As instructed, when we got to the chain-link gate, we honked.

The caretaker unlocked the gate, and as we drove in and parked, the air suddenly was filled with a beautiful sound. The wolves were singing a greeting to us with a chorus of howls.

Tonya Littlewolf led us inside the first enclosure, where we met the youngster, Istas Pejuta, and the 18-year-old elder of the pack, Apache Moon. We'd brought organic carrots and apples for them, and Istas wasn't shy about asking for some as Merry and Dave took pictures.

A high chain-link fence surrounded rocks, shrubs, a few small trees, and a "den" made of wood. There was room for them to run.

I discovered immediately that wolves' perspective on life is far different from that of domesticated animals. The pictures they sent me were filled with symbolism and what we might call mysticism and deep spirituality. I knew then that I would come back another day and spend time with each of these creatures to get the full impact of their wisdom.

But on this first visit, Istas was showing his youth. Tonya, who runs the non-profit sanctuary, informed us that his name means "Medicine Eyes" and that they often changed color "from blue ice green to yellow." But what we saw was a playful boy with blue eyes.

"There are things my eyes need to see and my ears need to hear," Istas said. "Everything is open to me, everything is free, and I need to show my spirit."

Apache, of course, had a different perspective. "I watch over the spirit of the young one," he said, "for he needs guidance, as I did when I was young. He gets so excited, he forgets his lessons. He is spoiled and needs to have manners.

"Anything that does not come from nature he wants to take. All of us want to do that," Apache explained, "because these things do not feel right to our touch or our eyes. They need to be hidden. But he needs to learn that some things need to be the way they are."

I didn't fully understand at the time what he was referring to, and it wasn't until we got to the last enclosure, which was occupied by cubs, that the issue became clear.

Meanwhile, Apache told me that he felt safe and loved, but he always looks "beyond."

"I am not longing to roam the openness," he said, "but rather I am in search of my kind, in hope they are as safe as I am.

"They have many miles to walk. I know those walks, for my pads have covered many kinds of soil. I have felt the softness of the green beneath my paws, and the wetness [dew] between the green that would encourage me to move on. I feel the heat change to cool as the dark comes, and I know the bright light [moon] will protect me and show me the way for all of my kind."

Apache had experienced many things in his long life, so he understood the difference between the safety he felt at that time and what other wolves encounter. That increased his worry about his brethren around the world.

"I am the keeper of the gate [for this pack]," he continued. "I protect the gate of danger, to keep us from a bad place. The moon is a spirit that protects me from the darkness."

Apache was just explaining that wolves' energy level depends on the phase of the moon when we were invited to move on to the next enclosure.

There we met the alpha Segoni, the healer Durango, and Dakota. Tonya instructed the visitors to line up around a large wooden platform, and the wolves leaped gracefully to the top of it. They greeted each of us, one at a time, by licking our faces and then rubbing their scent on us. We were now honored members of the pack, even though we were the "hairless ones."

Durango, who was pale with piercing golden eyes, was very knowledgeable about humans and the differences between the species.

"The body does not have pain or disease," he said. "It is only carried in the mind. Man sees through his mind and must label things out of fear. We see through our soul and know the spirit has no fear. You see illness and live by it, but that only encourages it to grow. We see health and we thrive on it.

"Man is never happy with what comes from the earth," Durango continued, "unless he put it there, never trusting the earth's own growth. But we have survived on it for health. You cover the earth with hard things, but we find comfort with the earth, for protection and warmth."

And then he said something that sent a chill down my spine: "We look across [mental telepathy] an open plane, waiting to hear the sound of one of our kind and hear the beauty in his voice. You hear that same sound and look for a way to silence it."

When I told Merry about the conversation, she informed me about the events taking place then in Alaska: hunters, riding in helicopters, were slaughtering wolves. I realized then that Durango knew what was happening there.

Dakota was next, and he provided some comic relief. He asked if I liked his face. I noticed that his body was light and his face dark, and none of the other wolves had a dark-colored face. I told him he had a great face and that he was an old soul, and he explained how he had come by this odd color combination.

"When I was old enough to come out of the den," Dakota said, "I backed out very slowly. The spirit of the light gave me the light body. But I was not ready to leave the safety of the den. My body was outside and my head stayed inside in the comfort of the dark for a while.

"I noticed the others were running, playing, and going in and out of the den, and I got a feeling this was a good thing. I was ready then, so I came all the way out. I still love being in my den. I cannot be seen because of the darkness of my face."

Dakota also revealed that he always paid attention to the hairless ones who had fur on their faces [men with beards], because they were like him.

I looked around and noticed that Segoni was lying on his side and that Nancy was kneeling over him. Tonya had said he had a tummy ache, and Nancy was doing some acupressure on him.

"I think I'm helping him," she said, as we walked to the next enclosure. There we met Blue and Niwah.

Blue was very wise and very deep, and his word-pictures were rich with imagery.

"My eyes long to see many things," he began." I long to see the wide arms of the great bird that once wrapped around itself and holds the feathers of the future close to its heart [the great spirit]. I long to feel the white [snow] under my feet, knowing it would lead me to safety when the light turned to dark. I long to see the white fall on my kind and stay upon the backs of the hunters [pack], all to stand as one.

"I know," he said, "that when one goes away by himself [to die] he will come back by himself [the soul returns in another].

Blue continued with his memories from the time when he was a cub. He showed me "the cold wet water that would cool down my tongue when the light was very hot. This would always be where we needed it to be. I could see the rocks [under clear water] but did not understand why the coolness was stopping me."

And he shared another memory with me: "The tall green ones [trees] did many things for us. When the light was hot, they would give us cool. When the great wind was strong, they would calm it down. When the water would come from above, they would keep us dry. They knew how to take care of us."

I was still thinking about Blue's pictures when we entered the final enclosure and met two dark-colored cubs, Wakinyan (male) and Shanta Wanagi (female), and a white female cub called Wana Chikal.

It was here that I finally understood Apache Moon's words about "things that need to be hidden."

Merry was wearing a hair clip, and as she sat down on a rock to get to wolf-eye level, each of the cubs told me they wanted to take the clip and bury it. Why? They said it was too shiny and had no smell. It didn't belong there. It needed to be buried so it couldn't be seen. But they were thwarted because they cherish fur, and the clip was in Merry's "fur." There was no way to remove it without insulting her. They stared at it and put their noses on it many times, but there was nothing else they could do.

In addition, Merry was chewing gum, and each of the cubs was attracted to the smell and tried to lick it out of her mouth, much to everyone's amusement.

Shanta said, "Why is it still in her mouth? Why doesn't she swallow it? Give it to me. I know what to do with it."

Merry managed to gently fend off the cubs' attentions, and we all had a good chuckle at the situation.

It turned out that the inhabitants of Wolf Mountain Sanctuary were content and knew they were safe and loved. That made me happy.

As we prepared to leave, Tonya shouted out a word in Apache and raised her arms as if to direct a choir. "That means sing for me," she explained.

SILENT WORDS

And from every section of the compound came that lovely chorus again, bidding us goodbye.

It's a day we'll never forget.

Chapter 17
It's All Happening at the Zoo

After our experience with the wolves, which reminded me that non-domesticated animals have a different view of the world than their tame brethren, we decided we should visit a zoo to get a more detailed perspective from other species.

Merry and I arrived at the zoo on an extremely hot August morning, intent on recording words and pictures. Large sections of the facility were under construction, including the entrance, so we did a lot of walking that day.

Our first encounter was with a meerkat, a small creature that looks somewhat like a prairie dog. He was standing atop a large rock, surveying the noisy crowd of children. Suddenly he turned his back on all of us and faced the sun.

I asked him why, thinking he was showing disdain for the onlookers.

"I am warming my stomach," he said, "and I am sitting tall so the light will warm all of my stomach. What do I care what they think? This is my place."

That sort of set the tone for most of the day. With a couple of notable exceptions, the animals were content with their environment and spent their time relaxing and doing whatever came naturally to them.

A few had jobs and were very pleased to do them. For example, the seals put on a show with their keepers during feeding time and loved demonstrating what they could do. They rolled over, they leaped out of the water and touched their snouts to overhanging poles, and they barked – all for handfuls of fish.

The oldest and biggest seal loved to be touched by his keeper.

"The more she touches me, the more I want to do things for her," he said. Then he bragged to the other two seals that he got to do more tricks because he was older.

One of the others said, "Just throw me the fish! I don't need to be touched."

And the third was quite impatient, repeating, "I'm ready! I'm ready! I'm waiting for my turn! When is it my turn?"

Their lively actions were in stark contrast to the sea lions languishing in a nearby enclosure. They lay on bare cement at the bottom of their pool area, waiting patiently for the cascading water to cover their bodies as the pool filled.

One told me he loved being half-covered, half in and half out of the water, as the liquid rose. I asked him if there was anything he didn't like, and he said he "missed the roughness" of real rocks. "Everything is smooth in here," he said.

When asked if he was scared when the water was gone, he replied that he was not because he knew the water would return. It was a perfect example of the way these animals adjust to whatever we need to do to care for them properly. He was content and he had three friends with him for company.

We were surprised to see the koala bear out in broad daylight, because we were under the impression that koalas are nocturnal creatures.

"I need to eat! I'm hungry right now!" he told me as he sat on a tree limb and wrestled with some tender, leafy branches. I noticed that he seemed to be most interested in the very tips of the shoots, so I asked him why.

"The ends are sweetest," he answered. "Sometimes I take the tips to them and share."

He was referring to the two wallabies who also occupied his enclosure, along with a porcupine and a peacock. The wallabies backed up the koala's story and were happy with his friendship and generosity.

The porcupine told me his job was to be on the ground, and whatever was there was his. "The others eat high," he said. When asked about his sharply pointed defense mechanism, he said, "I never use my quills. I don't need to. I'm safe here."

Mr. Koala lent credence to that statement. "When I go on the ground, he (the porcupine) leaves me."

We wondered why a peacock had been included in this particular mini ecosystem, but that question was soon answered.

"I'm here by accident," she said, "just for the day." I asked why she was lying flat on the ground with her feathers stretched out behind her, and she answered that she was just "drying her tail."

It was a peaceful scene occupied by innocent, peaceful little souls.

We climbed the hill to the lions' den and found a lioness half-sitting and half-lying in plain view. I said hello and asked if she would turn her face toward us.

She did, saying, "People look at me because they think I'm beautiful." She didn't mind. She was content.

The lioness got up and moved a few feet away and then laid down again. When asked why, she replied, "Because the ground is cooler." Such a simple answer.

The Lion King himself was half-hidden behind a small section of fence and tall bushes.

"I don't sleep here," he announced. "I like to be protected back here." In fact, he was quite upset that one bush had been removed, thus decreasing his privacy.

Although he was protective of her, the lioness said they had no offspring. "There are none of my kind being little," she said.

The two were quite comfortable in that setting, despite the fact that he was missing a bush and she had no hunting or child-rearing duties. They knew nothing else.

Right next door was perhaps the best exhibit at the zoo, a large enclosure featuring four giraffes. The shortest one was separated into a small area, and I asked him why.

"Because I am too little," he said. "I need to eat on my own."

It turned out that wasn't quite accurate, but it was his understanding of the situation.

The large male and two females were preoccupied with a hanging branch – suspended by the keepers from a small chain —

that offered some tender leaves. He did his best to turn the branch so the females could get to the shoots, but it was mostly an exercise in gentle patience.

We noticed that one of the females had a big tummy. She said she knew "something is there," but she didn't know what. "It was there before," she offered, and we guessed she was talking about the young male who was cordoned off from the others.

Every time she wondered if the little one was there, he would show himself to her. It was very sweet.

She explained that the big male and the little male were kept separated, but she didn't know why. When the small male was let into the large enclosure, the large male went into the small pen. It was difficult to tell how often this exchange took place.

At that point, the one we were now calling "Mom" walked daintily over to the large male and rubbed her neck on his. This example of silent affection was very touching.

The giraffes were sweet, easy-going, gentle creatures who were quite content in their environment.

We were anxious to see the elephants, so we walked down the hill toward their enclosure. On the way, I had planned to stop and communicate with gorillas, chimps, or any apes we could find. Unfortunately, all their exhibits were closed, and one zoo attendant told us there were no apes on the grounds. We were truly disappointed. I had anticipated some great conversations.

Only one elephant – a female – occupied that huge exhibit on that particular day. She was walking back and forth at a fairly rapid rate from one side to the other. I asked her why.

"Two times a day I move for the keeper," she explained, "and at each end I get a long orange thing or a little round red one."

I looked more carefully and saw the keeper placing carrots and apples through gated areas, and then I could see her consuming the fruits and vegetables.

"Then I get the green things," she said, as I watched some tender branches mysteriously appear under another gate.

After consuming her final treat, she walked to a covered area, telling me she wanted the keeper to spray her with the hose. It was difficult to know whether he did or not, but I suggested she take a dip in her elephant-sized pool.

And that she did, submerging herself next to an enormous tractor tire. "I like when the black thing rubs against me," she declared.

During our visit, she told me this was the third place she had been and she liked it the best because it was the biggest. When she thought about how she got to the first place, I could feel movement, as if she was in a boat.

She also said she had a male friend but she didn't know where he was right then.

I asked how she felt about her food and her environment in general.

"There is no looking here," she said. No one was going to steal her food. She felt safe and content.

We moved on to the California black bear exhibit, only to find a chain link fence and green tarps surrounding it. What a disappointment! But we could hear the zip of electric drills inside, so we peeked through some small holes in the tarp.

The bears were there! Unfortunately, so were some workmen who were welding an iron barrier fence, among other things.

Two bears paced back and forth, in and out of their cave, back and forth. They were extremely agitated and upset by the noise and the smells of the welding and other activities.

One asked me, "Are they leaving?"

I tried to reassure him. "Maybe two more darknesses," I said, "but it will be OK."

That didn't seem to appease him, but at least I was a momentary distraction.

"I am always safe in my cave," he said. "I can go in my cave, and I can go around and go in my cave." I perceived that the cave had two entrances.

"The water keeps me safe," he continued, referencing the waterfall and large pool separating his cave from the outer part of the enclosure where the men worked.

We felt so sorry for the bears because the situation was traumatic for them, and we wondered why they hadn't been moved while the work was done.

Worse yet, it was affecting the surrounding animals.

The tigers were right next door, and the male was so distraught by the noise and smells that he was trying to leave! He paced back and forth, looking for a way out, and more than once approached the water barrier and stuck his front paws into the drink.

"I must get out to end the noise!" he said.

I didn't know what to do to help him, so I spoke to the tigress, who was languishing under a tree. The sounds didn't bother her so much. I asked about her food.

"When the time is to eat, it is always there," she replied.

I had noticed quite a few squirrels on the grounds, so I asked her about them.

"They are not in my place," she said.

This innocuous conversation was going nowhere, so I stopped.

The plight of the bears and tigers was extremely upsetting for us, but we knew there was little we could do. The keepers were caring for the animals as usual, but we wondered why the creatures' emotional distress seemingly was not being taken into consideration. I wouldn't have been surprised to hear "Tiger escapes from zoo" on the 6 o'clock news.

Hoping that the small construction project would be short-lived, we moved on to the rhinoceros. I told him he was handsome, but he didn't know that concept. Instead, he was complaining about his mud holes. One was wet and one was dry, and he didn't understand why they both couldn't be wet. I figured he was just cranky because his enclosure was right across from the bears'.

He did have one positive thing to say, however: "The rocks are mine so I can move my body on it." He liked his rocks, and his armored suit showed signs of many "rubbings."

The rhino was one of many animals who disclosed that they did not sleep in the place where they were on view to the public. We wondered where.

Some of the more timid creatures, for example the small elk-like gerunds, were affected by the crowds. When a group of ebullient children swarmed toward their enclosure, the mini-deer hid behind some rocks.

"We don't like loud and fast," one told me. "We hide to protect ourselves."

As soon as the kids left, disappointed, the animals reappeared and began to show off for us. How gracefully they moved, all the while flicking their unique ears, the inside of which looked like a leaf pattern had been tattooed there.

It had been a long day, so we sadly left the zoo inhabitants behind. The most compelling impression I had was that these animals were all so innocent and so sweet. Every one I asked to turn and look at me (so Merry could take a photo) did so willingly.

They rely on humans to take care of them. They know nothing else, and they are mostly content, at least at this particular zoo.

I'm aware that some facilities exist where animals are not cared for properly, but I believe this is changing as zookeepers and the public become better educated.

SILENT WORDS

Chapter 18
Advice on Relationships

During all the years I've been communicating with animals, I have learned some practical concepts that help smooth our relationships with domestic companions. This can lead to a more peaceful household, which, on the whole, is a good thing. I thought I'd share a few of these practices with you here.

Mail and Newspapers
Many pets like to shred the mail and/or newspapers. They see you handling it, and they want to be part of the experience, so they feel compelled to get their paws and teeth on it.

Open a letter and give the envelope (or a page of the newspaper) to Fido. Tell him, verbally, that it's his mail/paper to read and the rest is yours. After a few repetitions, he'll get the idea, be pleased that you're sharing with him, and leave the rest alone. Just be sure he doesn't eat the newspaper, because ink can be toxic.

Christmas
How many times have you come home to find Christmas tree ornaments scattered around the room and wrapping and ribbons ripped off the presents? Or worse?

Not only do you have a mess, but your animal also could become ill from ingesting these items.

Again, the concept of sharing comes into play. That's all she wants.

At the same time you put up your Christmas tree, erect a colorful but small display in a corner. A green plastic bucket is ideal, because you can turn it upside down and it's sort of tree-shaped. Wrap some lights around it and make sure your animal knows this is *her* tree. Go back and forth between the two, decorating one and then the other.

Have her watch when you put presents around your tree and her gifts around her upside down bucket. Be sure her toys are wrapped in something safe, like unbleached tissue. Then you should both leave the room. You want to demonstrate that you're not opening your presents so she'll understand that she's not to touch hers either.

After some time has elapsed, return to the room together. Don't touch your tree or gifts when she's around, and keep an eye on her. Hopefully she will follow your example.

On Christmas morning, let her open her toys and treats first. Or, you can alternate. She'll make a small mess, but she'll have a great time, and, more importantly, she'll leave your packages alone.

There's a bonus: You can store her little "tree" decorations in the bucket!

This process might not work perfectly the first time around, but eventually she'll understand the concept.

On the subject of presents – and this goes for any gift-giving occasion – make your pet a part of the process. Many times we designate a present as being from an animal companion, so let her in on the fun!

If the person receiving the gift is part of the household, or will get the present when your pet is around, then make sure the animal knows the gift is from her. You can do this by leaving the package near her food bowl or on her bed for several hours before the occasion. Of course you'll need to explain she's not to touch it. When the time arrives, have her help you carry the present to the person and let her watch it being opened. She'll be delighted!

Animals totally understand the concept of gifts.

Food

Did you leave the hors d'oeuvres on a table that was accessible to Fido, and there were none remaining by the time your guests arrived? I can't guarantee it won't happen again if you leave food unattended, but I can help to make the regular dinnertime scenario more peaceful.

Domestic animals always ask if you'd like a bite of their food before they begin eating. Yes, it's true! They want to share. They're delighted if you "pretend" to take a mouthful before you put their bowl on the floor.

And they expect you to return the favor. As you sit down at the table, have a treat in your hand and pretend to take it off your plate. Give it to Fido and he will be satisfied that you have shared.

Diet

If your pet has continual skin problems, there's a good chance it's a food allergy. Read the label on the can or bag. "Meat by-products" is something you should avoid. Remember that trips to the vet for medical procedures are far more expensive than paying a little more for each meal! And if you decide to change the brand or type of food, do it *gradually* over two or three weeks. A sudden change will upset your animal's digestive system and perhaps cause even more problems.

While we're on the subject of food, let me stress that you should never give your dog a bone from *cooked* meat, with the possible exception of a large knuckle bone. The others are brittle and will splinter, and they can perforate the stomach and intestines. And, although they are popular, rawhide chews also can be dangerous. They can block the intestines.

One final note on food: a growing number of dog and cat breeders raise their animals on raw diets based on what wolves and big cats eat in the wild. The assumption is that domestic animals have the same enzymes as their ancestors and are thus not able to properly digest pre-packaged, cooked meals or kibble. In fact, the belief is that standard pet food can be toxic and will adversely affect animals' health, while the raw diet produces a higher percentage of disease-free pets. This alternative method is called the B.A.R.F. (biologically appropriate raw food) diet. It involves raw meat and bones (the ancestors' prey), along with raw vegetables and fruits (the prey's food). Before you try this, read about it online, or buy a book on the subject.

131

I do not use the B.A.R.F. diet, but I wanted you to be aware of this alternative. Merry, on the other hand, *does* feed her dogs raw. She claims they eat better than she does!

Trading

Most domestic animals understand the concept of trading, and they'll learn the meaning of the word "trade" in no time at all.

If she steals a book or a shoe or a pillow off the bed, don't run after her, yelling and demanding that the item be returned. Instead, be calm. Get a treat, hold it up for her to see, and offer to trade.

Yes, this can lead to stealing for the sole purpose of getting a treat! But they often steal for the sole purpose of getting your attention, anyway, so why not have a practice in place to avoid chasing after them?

This concept is particularly important when you discover your animal has something truly dangerous in her mouth. When "Leave it!" doesn't work, "trade" almost always does.

My Airedale, McKenzie, has actually taken trading to the next level.

He had never paid any attention to a stuffed "Snoopy" dog that languished on the back of the living room couch. Then one day I spotted McKenzie trotting out the sliding glass doors with Snoopy in his mouth.

I asked him to come to the living room with me, and there I saw another stuffed creature in Snoopy's old spot.

"Did you think I wouldn't notice?" I inquired.

"I traded," McKenzie responded, making me feel a little silly for misunderstanding. I learn something new from animals every day.

Leave It at the Door

Do you bring your work stress home with you? I can't tell you how many animals have sadly said that their owner is there in body but not in mind.

They are totally in tune to our mental stress and believe it is their purpose in life to ease our emotional strain, and they need to be reassured that they're doing their job.

No matter what, the very first thing you should do when you come home is greet and spend some time petting your animal companion.

The more time you spend, the less stressed you'll feel, because it really does work! They will take away your anxiety and frustration if you hold them close. So do yourself and your pets a favor. That's why it's called "petting!"

Sharing the Phone

A few of my clients had a problem with their dogs barking whenever they were on the phone. Most of the time, there is a simple solution.

Unless it's a business call, in which case you'd need to isolate yourself from the dog, you can simply ask the other party to participate.

Tell your caller the dog's name and ask him/her to speak to your companion for a minute. Then hold the phone to your dog's ear while your friend says a few words. Usually this works like a charm.

Again, your animal just wants to be included.

Be Calm

Because animals are so in tune with our emotions, if you get overly excited, speak loudly or yell in an animated fashion, your companion's energy level will automatically increase to equal yours.

That's why yelling at your pets frequently has the opposite effect from the one you desire.

You'll be much more successful in modifying their behavior if you are calm.

Illness

When animals get sick, they don't want to be a burden. If they think we're upset, their health will actually decline, so we can't let them know we're stressed.

Be calm and tell your pets it's OK to not feel well. Tell them "Now it's my turn to care for you!" Give them little treats, if possible, and spend time petting and reassuring them. Have a smile on your face and give them kisses.

I often think of Fuzz, an older Golden Retriever who swallowed a barbeque brush with metal bristles. He hid his growing physical distress from his owners until it was almost too late. The thin strands had already perforated his intestines and he developed peritonitis.

Fuzz spent two weeks in the hospital and underwent three surgeries. His owners visited at least once a day, calmly feeding him little bits of chicken, petting and kissing him and telling him it was OK. Lots of love, combined with positive thinking, worked wonders. He pulled though just fine. The vets were very skilled, but Fuzz would have crossed over anyway if he thought he was being a burden.

A New Family Member

When you bring home a new puppy or kitten, or a rescue animal, the usual practice is to also bring home a collar, toys, and a food bowl.

If you already have an animal at home, he needs to be included in these exciting events. Make sure you also bring home new toys, collar and bowl for him so he feels like he's part of the activities and has not lost his place in the household (or in your hearts).

You'll need to help your puppy adjust to her new environment, especially the sounds. Drop things on the floor and then let her investigate the items. She'll soon see that they're harmless. Turn on the vacuum cleaner and then turn it off so she can approach and sniff it. Turn it back on and move it, and then turn it off and leave it again.

After a while, she won't be frightened because it will become a familiar sound in her new home.

Your kitten or puppy also needs to be held and cuddled to make it easier for the vet and groomer. Play with her paws, look in her mouth, and rub her tummy so she'll become accustomed to being handled.

In addition, socialization is important for dogs. Take your puppy on walks and let him interact with other people and canines. This will make him less fearful of new situations. Fear can cause aggression, and I'm sure you'd much rather your dog be friendly! An obedience class also is an excellent way to socialize your pup, as is taking him to a dog park if you have one in your town.

Keep in mind that puppies and kittens frequently are "out of control." Don't expect them to behave like adults. They will break things, have accidents, chew on various items, and nip and scratch you. Be patient with them, because they're worth every destroyed slipper or shredded curtain.

The Groomer

Choose your groomer carefully. Your pet could be traumatized or even injured by improper handling. Get a recommendation from your vet or good friends, or watch the groomer work. If s/he appears not to be a loving "animal person," go elsewhere.

And speaking of groomers, consider providing some heat relief to your pets. If you have a long-haired cat or dog that is not a show animal, a little shave might be much appreciated during the summer months. A good groomer will know how to do this properly.

If you bathe your animals yourself, you'll no doubt be interested in this story:

A client of mine has a long-haired cat who faints when he is bathed. He goes completely limp and seems to lose consciousness. When she takes him out of the bath and rubs him with a towel, he's just fine. He told me he doesn't like to be bathed, so this is his way of avoiding the experience. He's just playing possum. So if it happens to you with your cat, don't be alarmed.

The Need to be Needed

Animal companions need to feel they are needed and have important jobs, even if their job is just to take away your daily stresses.

If you make dogs or cats stay outdoors, or don't visit your horses very often at the stable, there's a good possibility they will not feel needed because they're not in contact with you enough to do their jobs.

The next thing that happens will often be a pet who does something dramatic to get your attention: chewing up your favorite shoes or book, having an "accident" in the house, or getting sick.

Vacation Blues

Do your pets become anxious when you're away on vacation? Here's a way to reassure them that you have not abandoned them. It will give you some peace of mind as well.

When you feed him the last meal before you depart, use a new, brightly colored bowl. Explain that the next time he sees that bowl, you will be returning home before the next meal.

Be sure your pet sitter or the kennel knows about this arrangement and follows through. You might want to make a call as a reminder.

Another thing you can do to reassure your pet while you're gone is to leave some slept-in T-shirts around the house so he can snuggle up to your scent. If you'll be absent for more than a few days, put extra T-shirts in a plastic bag to preserve the scent. Your pet sitter can then distribute them over a period of time. The same can be done in his crate at the kennel.

Ice Water

Animals prefer their bowls to be filled with fresh *cold* water. If it's a hot day, throw in some ice cubes. If you'll be absent for a while, freeze a larger block of ice to drop in the bowl.

Divorce

How do your animals feel in a joint custody situation after a divorce? They're actually OK with it. But there is one thing you can do to make conditions more comfortable for them.

Initially, their bowls, beds and toys should be transported with them as they travel back and forth. Once they are used to splitting time in different places, new items can be purchased by the person who has the animals the least number of days.

But before all of this can happen, one of you will be moving, and moving can be as traumatic for animals as it is for humans.

Moving

Watching you pack up boxes can be tremendously distressing to your pets, especially if they don't fully understand what is happening.

Do not pack before you have found your new home. Once you have located it, picture it in your mind; and be sure to picture your pets with you in the new place, so they'll know they're coming with you. Take them on a virtual tour to give them some idea what to expect in their new surroundings. *Then* you can pack.

And while you're packing, continue to picture them with you in their future home. This will reassure and calm them and also have a good influence on their behavior.

Keep in mind that if you're not happy with your new abode, your pets won't be happy either. Choose wisely.

And once you have moved to a new location, take your dog on walks around the neighborhood as soon as possible. He'll want to see and smell his new territory. If you don't do the walks, he might escape and do them by himself!

Training

If you have approached your training sessions properly, your dog will associate the word "good" – and your accompanying cheerful voice – with pleasure and rewards.

Your dog also will know such commands as "sit," "come," and "leave it." When she obeys, instead of saying "good girl," reinforce WHY she has pleased you by saying "good sit!" or "good stay!"

You'll be surprised at the difference it makes and how much it will speed up the training process.

One final thing: A dog trainer I know once said that the command "come" should be rewarded with great jubilation and many treats, because it is the most important command. It is what will keep your dog out of danger. "Come," he said, "should be like Christmas!"

Common Sense

You'd be amazed at some of the things people do without thinking.

If your cat has been under the bed for four days and refuses to eat, don't call me! Get him out of there immediately and take him to the vet.

Buy a crate based on the size a dog will be when she's fully grown, not the size she is as a puppy.

When you're looking to buy a new vehicle, measure the inside to make sure there's room for crates, beds, cages, etc. Your animals will need to be transported, and they deserve to travel in comfort and safety.

If you're thinking of adopting an animal companion, use some common sense. You need a pet that fits your environment and your lifestyle. Cats, for the most part, will adapt to any loving home, but dogs do not. Research the various breeds and learn about the personality characteristics and needs of each one before you make a decision. And keep in mind that an "all-American dog" usually is more anxious to please.

You'd be surprised how many dogs escape their yards because the gardener or pool man or meter reader forgot to shut the gate.

Know when these people are coming and keep your animal in the house on those days.

Cat Carriers

Is it a struggle to get your furry friend into the cat carrier to take her to the vet? No surprise. Every time she gets in it, she ends up at the vet. So, make the cat carrier part of her everyday life. Leave it in the living room, with the door open, and toys and treats and a pillow inside. Eventually she will get curious, go in, and discover that nothing bad happens as a result. Then take her in it to places that are fun. She'll associate it with adventure, not the vet.

Want to Try Visualization?

Are you ready to try behavior modification through visualization? If so, remember to keep in mind that your animal is constantly monitoring your mood and the pictures accompanying your thoughts.

Start in a closed, quiet room with no distractions. Ask your dog to sit-stay on the opposite side of the room.

Clear your mind and focus. Picture your animal coming toward you – from HIS perspective. That is the key! Put yourself mentally in his paws and visualize what he would be seeing if he got up and walked toward you. Remember that he is much shorter than you are, so you'll need to sit on the floor to actually "see" what he would be seeing.

Did it work? Did he come to you? If so, be sure to express your pleasure by saying "good come!" and giving him a treat and many kisses.

When you're working with your animal on behavior issues, keep in mind that there are no pictures for a negative. If you want him to stop doing something, then you must picture what you want him to do *instead*. If you "see" him doing the wrong thing, then he will continue to do it because that's the message you're sending. Find a way to distract him by picturing him engaging in a different activity… from his perspective, of course.

The visualization process can have many applications, as you might imagine. A friend of mine uses it to train her horse in dressage. She tried picturing what she wanted him to do from her perspective, but that didn't work. It wasn't until she focused on what HE would see that he began to respond correctly.

Keep trying! There's no limit to what you can achieve when you learn to communicate with your animals using mind pictures. Just don't expect to get any images back! However, if you do receive an occasional flash from your pet, don't panic. It can be a startling experience, but it just means you are on the same "wavelength" at that moment and you are much more receptive than most humans. That's a good thing!

Letting Go

When an animal is ready to cross over to the other side, be unselfish. No matter how much you love him, it's time to let go.

"If you love me, set me free."

Chapter 19
Awareness

One of the best ways to keep your pets happy and safe is to stay aware. Pay attention and listen to your intuition.

My friend Mary took Princess to a national dog show. As she watched Princess and her handler in the ring, Mary's impression of the judge was that she was a very tall woman with a big dark hat. Mary knew, somehow, that Princess was having a problem with that hat.

After the competition, the handler said when the judge approached, Princess had stiffened up and "didn't want that woman to touch her."

When I asked Princess about it later, she showed me the judge from her perspective. She looked about 10 feet tall, which was exactly the vision she had sent to Mary. And Mary, without realizing that the picture had come from Princess, had seen the same thing. However, although Mary sensed there was a problem with the hat, she couldn't clearly comprehend what the problem was.

Princess showed me the hat. Animals see auras, the colors of the energy fields that emanate from people. I see these auras when animals show me pictures of them.

The judge's hat was holding in her aura, keeping it in like a pressure cooker. Princess knew there were supposed to be colors; but there were none, so she wanted nothing to do with that individual.

Two good lessons can be learned from this experience. First, trust your intuition, because what you see in your mind's eye might be a message from your pet. Second, always keep in mind that animals don't see things the way we do, literally or figuratively. And their behavior frequently is based on what they see.

They always have, at least in their minds, a perfectly good reason for whatever they do. Does your pup bark at the handyman fixing something in your house? You can bet she sees the wrong colors in his aura, colors that indicate, at the very least, a bad mood.

Sometimes animals exhibit behavior that seems out of character. For instance, a show dog was perfectly sweet and gentle, until he was put in his crate. He would then become what is called "crate aggressive" and snarl at almost anyone who came near him. People who saw him under those circumstances believed he had temperament problems, but such was not the case. You see, he had previously been boarded with a professional handler who kept him in a crate most of the time. Aside from the fact that it was extremely cruel, it also created in him the belief that his crate was his "den," and therefore it had to be defended at all cost. Despite the fact that he had been with a new handler for a year and was not crated at home, he still had that mentality. Sadly, that is the case with most dogs we see barking and growling at shows. They spend entirely too much time in their crates.

On the more positive side, a mischievous dog might be trying to distract and entertain you in order to take your mind off whatever is worrying you. Or, he might have an entirely different reason.

Here's a perfect example:

I have some plants in a basket on my dining room table. Every so often, I put the basket in the sink and water the plants; and after they've drained, I bring the basket back to the table. One day McKenzie observed this process. The next thing I knew, he was struggling to bring a large leafy bush branch through the sliding glass doors.

He worked and worked, finally learning through trial and error that the limb had to come through the long way. He laid the branch under the dining room table.

When I asked him why he had done this, he explained that he wanted to put his "green" with my "green." I broke off an appropriately sized piece and put it with my other plants, and he was delighted.

They always want to be a part of what is happening, so it's best to stop and think about what their motivation might be, rather than react with anger or dismay.

You *should,* however, react with dismay if you happen to see an animal being mistreated. I'm certainly not suggesting that you spy on your neighbors, because most people have pets because they love them. But there's always the occasional sociopath who will abuse animals. Call the Humane Society immediately!

The shelters are filled with dogs, cats, bunnies, etc. who have been injured or neglected by humans. The Animal Planet network airs several series dealing with those who rescue these poor creatures. It happens. And it's up to us to be aware and report what we witness to the proper authorities. The Humane Society will not reveal your name.

Although it's a chilling subject, I would be remiss if I didn't mention that nearly every serial killer on record tortured animals as a child. If you see that kind of serious incident, be a good citizen and either speak gently to the child yourself or try to talk to the parents. If you're not comfortable doing that, then call the Humane Society.

We also need to be aware that the most frequently seen example of animal mistreatment is usually unintentional: leaving a dog in the car with the windows rolled up on a hot day. The owners are either uneducated on the subject or their intention is to "just run into the store for a minute." If you witness this and the owners are nowhere in sight, you need to act quickly, because the dog could die in a very short period of time. If the car doors are locked, call the fire department and then try to find the owner in nearby stores or homes.

Your awareness could save an animal's life, and not just in an emergency situation.

As I've said before, your pets constantly monitor your emotions because it's their job to relieve your stresses. If you have something in the back of your mind that won't go away – because it's a circumstance you cannot control – then that will have a long-term effect on your animals. It could eventually affect their health if they feel they've had no success in alleviating your worries.

143

Examples would be 9/11, the tsunami, the war, upsetting events you see on the news, hurricane devastation, and other things of that nature. You have no control over those incidents, but they stay on your mind nevertheless. When thousands of lives are lost, or even a precious few, the world feels unbalanced.

Here's how you can help your pets deal with these unsettling images. Concentrate and picture the event taking place just *outside* your property. Then picture you and your animals *inside*, all warm and cozy and safe. Repeat the process until you're sure you've made your point. This is your way of telling them that what happens outside the home should not concern them.

And since the incidents are beyond your control, you'd be doing yourself a favor, too, if you'd *"Leave It"* at the door!

About the Authors

CINDY WOOD has been a working animal communicator for nearly 40 years and has clients around the world. Many she has never met in person, because she has the ability to connect with animals from long distances. She often helps rescue organizations determine the reasons for animals' behavior so they can be placed in appropriate homes, and she has been called in to help with hundreds of lost animal cases. Most of her work, however, is done in clients' homes, where animals feel comfortable. Cindy Wood Consultations can be reached at 818-842-0994.

Merry Shelburne has a M.A. degree in mass communications and is the author of a public relations textbook that is still being used in college classrooms in several countries. She is a former college journalism professor, a retired college public information officer, and a writer, photographer, graphic artist, and online shopkeeper. She and her husband and their two Golden Retrievers spend weekends at dog agility trials.

Made in the USA
San Bernardino, CA
27 July 2019